A Living Buddhism for the West

A LIVING BUDDHISM FOR THE WEST

Lama Anagarika Govinda

Translated by
Maurice Walshe

SHAMBHALA
Boston & Shaftesbury
1990

Shambhala Publications, Inc.
Horticultural Hall
300 Massachusetts Avenue
Boston, Massachusetts 02115

Shambhala Publications, Inc.
The Old School House
The Courtyard, Bell Street
Shaftesbury, Dorset SP7 8BP

9 8 7 6 5 4 3 2 1

First Edition
Printed in the United States of America on acid-free paper
Distributed in the United States by Random House
and in Canada by Random House of Canada Ltd.
Distributed in the United Kingdom by Element Books Ltd.

Library of Congress Cataloging-in-Publication Data
Govinda, Anagarika Brahmacari.
[Buddhismus für das Abendland. English]
A living Buddhism for the West/Lama Anagarika Govinda: translated by Maurice Walshe—1st ed.
p. cm.
Translation of: Buddhismus für das Abenland.
ISBN 0-87773-509-3
1. Buddhism—Doctrines. I. Title.
BQ4150.G6813 1990 89–43318
294.3—dc20 CIP

Contents

Editor's Foreword vii
1. Perspectives of Buddhism in the World Today 1
2. The Meaning of Insight, Knowledge, and Wisdom in Buddhism 30
3. The Role of Morality in the Maturing of the Human Personality 54
4. The Bodhisattva Ideal: A Light in the Darkness of Our Time 72
5. The Meaning of Ritual, Liturgy, and Initiation in Buddhism 94
6. Guru and Chela 107
7. The Introspective Paths in Buddhism and Their Significance for Humanity Today 124

CLEVELAND H. PARDUE, III, M.D.
465 ST. MICHAELS DRIVE, SUITE 202
SANTA FE, NM 87505

(505) 994-0303 LIC. # ____________

NAME ____________ AGE ______

ADDRESS ____________ DATE ______

℞

April 11
→ May 30.

Crane Burnett

ELEEMOSYNARY

Refill ______ times

(Signature)

To ensure brand name dispensing, prescriber must write 'No Substitution' or 'NO SUB' on the prescription.

9DOB1374497

April 11
→ May 30.
Grace Barnett

Editor's Foreword

One of the greatest modern interpreters, thinkers, and meditation masters in the field of Buddhism has departed from us. Lama Anagarika Govinda left this life on 14 January 1985, in his eighty-sixth year, clearly conscious and with a smile on his lips.

Not long previously, he had made the final corrections to the manuscript of this book, and had declared that his work on it was finished. This was the culmination of three years of intensive work on the various chapters, which he continually rewrote, repeatedly discussing their contents with his most intimate circle of pupils and seeking their criticisms, in order to bring out more and more clearly the points that he considered essential.

The origins of this book are rather unusual. In the course of a visit to the United States, I had urged Lama Govinda to provide a spiritual testament for his Ārya Maitreya Maṇḍala Order—that is, for that close circle of disciples whom he always regarded as the heirs and continuers of his work. He agreed. It was to be a short essay in which he would earnestly remind his chelas that this family (*kula*), this "brotherhood of heart and mind," which was based on a previously existing affinity between its members, would only justify its existence in the future if it always remained conscious of its purpose, which was to devote all its energies to the furtherance of Buddhism in the present time. In this context he asked us what seemed to us to be the most essential part of his work, what part of it might be useful to mankind for a further period of time, and how the message of the Buddha-Dharma should be presented to the present age with a view to the future.

Accordingly, various members of the order collected material with these points in mind. Notebook entries, extracts from letters, essays, notes of lectures and conversations, interviews, and hastily scribbled notes by Lama Govinda were arranged by subject matter, collected together, and laid before him. Much of what we had gathered together he rejected as "immature," "superseded," or "only partly right," and he replaced some of it with ideas that were new, and often revolutionary, to us.

He declared that the principal purpose of this book must be to reveal the dynamism of the Buddha-Dharma through the millennia: that inherent dynamism that the Dharma has displayed again and again when manifesting as a creative and transforming force in the most varied cultures and social systems, as well as in times in which orthodoxy and scholasticism threatened to stifle all genuine religious experience. This was the meaning of the task given to him by his teacher Tomo Geshe Rinpoche, and which he entrusted to his own pupils and successors: to work untiringly at developing all their own potential powers, in order to put these entirely at the disposal of all living beings, to present the Buddha-Dharma in an interpretation adequate to the understanding of the age and, further, to develop methods of meditation that are practicable for people under the conditions of present-day society. At the same time, the order must always bear in mind its own particular path: while learning from the experience of past millennia, we must proceed on our way as the Ārya Maitreya Maṇḍala, developing the essential features of that way while never forgetting that our way is only one among the many possible ways within the Dharma, all of which are directed at the same goal.

Very soon, however, Lama Govinda felt the need to widen the scope of the original plan for the book, which seemed to him to be too restricted. And so, during the joint work on this book the idea arose in him to make it, as his testament, something that addressed itself not merely to his narrow band of pupils in the Ārya Maitreya Maṇḍala, but also to his friends all over the world. It should be an expression of what he most sought to do: to inspire and stimulate all those who have ventured on the perilous and adventurous path of the spirit. He wanted in this way to make a contribution toward the creation of a world in which humanity and universal responsibility toward the whole of life occupy a central place, and in which there is sufficient room at the same time for the individual development of the potential of those human beings who are conscious of being bound up in the network of infinite, mutually conditioning relationships. For, according to Lama Govinda's conviction, it is only through such a new consciousness that we can confront the danger of the creeping destruction of all life—a danger arising from the measureless expansion of demands and greeds—and counter it before it destroys all the prerequisites of life on this earth: water, air, the earth, and all sources of nourishment, as well as the whole symbiosis of the animal and vegetable kingdoms, which would also make impossible the path to enlightenment.

Lama Anagarika Govinda is no longer an unknown figure. His books and lecture tours made him one of the most prominent representatives of a future-oriented Buddhism, and also an exponent of the New Age. From his earliest youth he always felt the urge to harmonize his thinking, feeling, and acting, to discover discrepancies quickly and eliminate them. In so doing he consistently followed his inner direction, without losing his mental openness to everything that was new and valuable in art and science, always prepared to meet new experiences and to empathize with humans and animals alike. Borne along on the living flood of his inner experiences, his world-picture never crystallized in final form, but was—like himself—always "on the way of the white clouds" and, like these, in a state of continual transformation. Thinking was for him "contemplative thinking" in Goethe's sense, and more, a principle of ordering *experienced* contents. Creative, intuitive thought such as he required from his chelas did not move in a realm of bloodless abstractions and concepts, but in the imaginative apperception and experiencing of the present, which, it seemed to him, should, magnetlike, draw to itself our whole devotion and attention.

For him it was a dominant feature of our time that the functions of sense perception were becoming progressively atrophied through the one-sided development and favoring of abstract thought, which, when separated from the images that enable us to convey and reexperience life directly, causes our mental and spiritual life to petrify as dogmatics, scholasticism, and traditionalism.

Accordingly, Lama Govinda was sharply opposed to the imitation of forms that had developed in past times and under different cultural conditions. His aim was an *assimilative* reshaping in order to set free a creative process that will never end as long as human beings strive for the highest goal. It is necessary, while taking one's stand firmly on the foundations established in the past, to work in the present with an eye to the future, responsibly, in the spirit of the bodhisattvas.

Such an inner directedness, however, can only come to be within us when we have matured into a meditative attitude to life that accompanies and supports our daily existence and that, therefore, is not some kind of "exceptional situation" in the course of our daily activity. For it is only when meditation is the expression of continuous present awareness that its transforming power can exert itself. Only then can we experience the totality of our human existence in its physical, mental, and spiritual complexity as an ever renewed, processual flow of occurrence bound up with the transcending universal in the unity of all that is coming to be, and which without exception is called to perfect enlightenment, liberation, and buddhahood.

• • •

My thanks go to all members of the order who contributed to the making of this book by collecting and arranging potential material.

My special thanks go to Dr. and Mrs. Laucker for their great help and constructive criticism, and to Śraddhamālā, who uncomplainingly retyped fair copies of manuscripts after repeated revisions.

I further wish to express personal thanks to Vajramālā, Vajrācāryā AMM, for her never-failing assistance over a period of three years.

ADVAYAVAJRA

1 | *Perspectives of Buddhism in the World Today*

Religions cannot be created intellectually. They grow according to their indwelling universal laws, just as a plant grows. They are natural revelations of the spirit, in which the individual shares. But their conformity to universal laws does not necessarily mean that their product is the same. These same laws, in fact, operate so as to produce different forms and contents under different conditions. Accordingly, from the standpoint of comparative religion, we can always only speak of a parallelism, never of an identity of religious ideas. In fact it is precisely where the same words and symbols are used in different religions that their underlying meaning is often quite different. Identity of form never guarantees an identity of content, because the meaning of these forms always depends on the particular associations connected with them. These associations vary, however, according to the particular historical, cultural, and civilizational soil from which they have grown.

Thus it is as senseless to try to bring all religions under a common denominator as it would be to try to overlook the differences between the plants and trees in a garden, or to ascribe these to an imperfect way of viewing them. Just as the beauty of a garden consists precisely in the extent and variety of its trees and flowers, each having its own particular kind of perfection, so too the garden of the spirit derives its beauty and life from the multiplicity and variety of its forms of experience and expression. And just as the communal life of a garden consists in the fact that all the trees and plants grow from the same soil, breathe the same air and reach out toward the same sun, so too all religions, with all their various schools, grow out of the same soil of inner reality and are nourished by the same cosmic powers. This is what they have in common.

But their character and their particular beauty—in which their inner worth consists—depend on those features in which they differ from one another, and which enable them to appear perfect in a unique way. Therefore, we should never try to simply explain away the differences between religions or between their schools; neither should we trivialize these, or describe them as mistaken interpretations or misunderstandings, merely in order to attain to some abstract "agreement" or even "absolute unity" that is then declared to be the "sole reality." Such an attempt can be destructive and fatal for the spirit of religion, just as it would be death to art if we wanted to dictate to the artist how he was to represent nature. For it is a sign of true art that artists painting the same landscape create a different picture in each case. Yet it is just this difference of artistic conception that gives every work of art its own value. Uniqueness and originality are signs of genius in every sphere of life—and indeed of life itself. On the other hand, sameness and standardization are signs of mechanization, mediocrity, and spiritual stagnation.

Religions are the expression of supraindividual inner experiences established over long periods of time, which possess a higher community through which they share in a universal consciousness. They find their decisive form of expression and their realization in the most highly developed and sensitive spirits, which possess the ability to share in the supraindividual life of their fellow human beings. Thus, religion is more than just a "collective thinking and feeling," which latter is a sign of artificially created and organized mass movements and thus is not a part of the supraindividual consciousness, but must on the contrary rather be ascribed to the subindividual level of the herd mentality.

Being the forms of expression of supraindividual experiences, religions—like everything else in the world—are subject to continual change, which however follows a particular direction in accordance with the tendency inherent in each one. Since the capacity for such transformation is the expression of the living dynamism of a given religion, the continuity and life of that religion are ensured for as long as this dynamism remains alive in certain individuals. This works against the stagnation and hardening of the dogmatic arteries in petrified forms of organization that lead to the cessation and death of all immediate experience, and hence of all religiosity.

If we consider the existence of an individual, we see that life in all its forms (from the embryo through birth to maturity and death) is characterized by an unbroken process of assimilation. "Nutriments" are continually taken in—whether in the form of concrete nutrition, water, and air, or in the form of transmitted experiences, modes of behavior, and thought—and these are broken down, in the organism, into their constituents and absorbed as such, to be transformed into part of the body substance, or to subjective trains of thought and mental structures. Whatever is unacceptable or superfluous to the body's requirements is excreted; "dead matter" that once formed part of the organism is likewise dissolved, the useless being eliminated and that which can be still used being "recycled."

But just as a living organism is experienced as a whole despite its constantly changing nature, so too religions, because of their intuitive character born of the unity of experience, are always a single whole, something perfect in itself throughout all changes. In this they are contrasted with science, which in view of its dependence on the knowledge and interpretation of external facts at any given time must always remain something incomplete and fragmented, a fact that in the past used to lead to relatively frequent changes of direction.

The transformation of forms and doctrinal interpretations to which all the great religions have been subject in the course of history, on the other hand, still clearly reveals the retention of a certain basic tendency; thus all the transformations undergone by any religion are regularly characterized by a shift of stress within the tendencies already existing in that religion. This may become necessary, on the one hand, because the religion has penetrated into differently structured cultural circles and civilizations, with the result that the religious and social background of these is also altered in the course of the process of assimilation. Or, on the other hand, changes in the social structures of those cultural circles in which a religion has taken root may produce characteristic variants, as can also happen through a change in the perception of the world due to scientific research.

The fact that during and after such a process of transformation there are always people and groups who cling to the old is so in part because these people are still living in the consciousness of a past age, which they idealize in order to escape from the present. Another reason is the fact that in all human beings resistance to change and lethargy initially oppose any changes, so that they may continue to live according to comfortable old patterns of behavior.

True religiosity, however, is based on a religious experience that opens up, born of devotion, which bears all the marks of spontaneity and whose principal motivating factor is that urge in man to outgrow himself. Therefore a religious person is not one who believes in particular dogmas or who is convinced of the truth of certain doctrines or follows certain moral prescriptions, but rather one who possesses the strength, the ability, and the will to sacrifice, thereby opposing the inborn natural tendency to egoism. Thus religion is not a "means" but—like life itself—bears its meaning in itself. It is a spiritual form of life, an individual intensification of consciousness on a suprapersonal basis. It is of the nature of religion that it lifts the individual out of his solitude in order to become a communal being and—after further progress—a cosmic being.

Judgments such as "good" and "bad" have nothing to do with religion as such. Morality is at best a by-product of religious life, never the goal of religion. Moral people are often totally irreligious, whereas nonmoral people are often astonishingly religious. Therefore the equation of religion with morality was one of the most fateful errors of mankind. It degraded religion to the level of a policeman, until even the finest people became confused. The antireligious attitude of the West is principally due to this error, compounded by the equation over a period of sexuality with immorality.

It was out of this attitude that there arose the contemptuous attitude toward aboriginal, "primitive" religions as so-called "lower forms" of the religious life, whereas in fact even the fetishism of Central African Negroes or of South Sea Islanders untouched by modern civilization, or the shamanism of primitive Asiatic tribes, is from the point of view of religious intensity (i.e., from that of religious experience and inward devotion) to be rated considerably higher than many forms of religion existing in the world today.

The greatest danger that has always threatened all religions, however, comes from the representatives of their organized communities. These people, whose experience is only at second hand—a surrogate "experiencing" of conceptually fixed dogmas and orthodox concepts, bound to the letter of "sacred books"—are the ones who put a block on all religious experience that does not agree with the principles of faith on which they remain fixated.

These dogmatically fixed ideas were certainly justified once from a historical point of view, but in the meantime they have become degraded into mere superstitions. Through these traditionalists and fundamentalists, all the great religions drag around a ballast, in the form of their sacred scriptures and traditions, of dated and historically long outlived material that was and remains an essential factor in the *development* of the religion in question but that from the point of view of the present-day religious seeker, is as useless as the ideas of early childhood are for an adult human being.

People in the West have today largely become more critical and more mature. Youth in particular is no longer willing to be fobbed off with dogmas and articles of faith, whether political, social, or religious in nature. In the religious sphere especially, young people seek ways that will enable them to have religious experiences of their own. Sadly, in so doing they often fall into the hands of charlatans and fanatics from the East as well as the West, and finally merely replace one sterile creed with another.

It is time for people to wake up and realize that the great religions have collected many things at a superficial level in the course of centuries, things that were significant for these religious movements at particular points in their history. But we, as people of our time, should recognize that it is not our task either to imitate the forms of past ages or to take over without question thought patterns that were once valid but are now outmoded. Rather we should try to extract from a doctrine everything that is relevant to our own time. The point is to distill the *essence* for our own daily practice and meditation, while recognizing what is outmoded for what it is: the record of previous stages that led to the religious, social, and cultural situation of the present time.

But just as the temples of the present rise upon the ruins of the temples of the past, which serve as their foundation, so too we must move forward. In the course of our evolution as human beings, we have had to leave behind us many ideas and thought patterns that were once very important for this development. Whoever wants to march forward must cast away the ballast of the past, even if this was once an important factor in the development which led to the present situation. This is an adaptation of what the Buddha taught us in regard to the Dharma: the Dharma, he said, is a raft, a means of reaching another and better shore, which we should then leave behind without clinging to it when it has fulfilled its function.

After the East was closed to Western thought for almost fifteen hundred years and revealed its wisdom only to a handful of initiates from the outside world, a movement is now becoming evident that is diametrically opposed to the spirit of Eastern teaching, and which clearly points to a weakening of the religious sense. I refer to the urge to convert and proselytize. This urge, which was previously a monopoly of the monotheistic religions of Western Asia and was quite unknown to the religions of India and the Far East, arises from the will to power and often from a spiritual uncertainty that lays store in the number of fellow believers that can be counted: the individual feels strengthened in his own faith the more it is shared by other people.

On the other hand, where there is certainty resulting from inner experience, it is of no consequence how many people accept a faith or reject it. For just as nobody needs to make converts to the proposition that twice two makes four, and just as there has never been a missionary for mathematics—the methods and results of which are evident—so too the wise men of the past considered their insights to be self-evident and therefore had no need to make propaganda for their wisdom. They only passed it on to those who showed themselves worthy to receive it, who understood it and could experience it for themselves, and who were willing to make sacrifices and to exert all their strength to that end. These people had to possess a certain degree not only of maturity but also of impartiality; that is to say, they had to be people who came with the necessary capacity to open up inwardly so that they could experience and realize the truth of these insights within themselves, without succumbing to any sort of suggestive indoctrination.

This attitude has been that of Buddhism from the very beginning. The Buddha himself displayed his teaching to all and appealed to all who could take it in, but he never used either physical or spiritual force in order to convince people of the truth of his worldview and the correctness of his path. He declared everything openly, and whoever came was welcome. Anyone who passed by and failed to accept it was neither scorned nor depreciated, and was not exposed to mental pressure by the threat of eternal damnation. In consequence of this basic attitude, Buddhism spread over the whole of the then known world of Asia, thus embracing the majority of people living in this continent. If we want to present Buddhism for the world of today, especially for the world of the West, we must adopt the same inner attitude. Buddhism must never become an instrument of power in the hands of great prelates or priests, however venerable these may be. It must present to all people the simple wisdom and truth of the Enlightened One and of all those great beings who followed in his footsteps and realized it for themselves in order to reinterpret it for their own times.

When, more than fifty years ago, the Ārya Maitreya Maṇḍala Order was founded at the instigation of our first patriarch, the Venerable Tomo Geshe Ngawang Kalzang, this attitude was laid down as its basis. It was not to be an organization for converting those of other faiths, but a brotherhood of mind and heart, ready to help those who had been inspired by the teachings of the Buddha and who wanted to put it into practice as human beings of our time.

And then, when the order took form in the West twenty years later, this was a spontaneous development born of an inner need and not the result of propagandist activity. The aim of our order was from the very beginning to maintain the living tradition of Buddhism as it had been passed down for thousands of years from guru to chela, by continually realizing it anew in our daily life. At the same time we were clear from the beginning that this can only happen in conformity with the demands of the age, within the framework of the social conditions under which we live, and also in common with all those who want to tread the bodhisattva path and who have been initiated into the teachings and meditation practices of the "direct path" of Vajrayāna.

Prior to the appearance of the Ārya Maitreya Maṇḍala in the West, most Buddhist groups in the West—with few exceptions—consisted of organizations whose main aim was to convince people intellectually of the rationality of the Buddha's teaching. Such a procedure was undoubtedly necessary as a first step toward the understanding of Buddhism. But very few people proceeded beyond that point. We were and are convinced that the second step must necessarily follow the first, because only in this way can Buddhism be recognized as the spiritual force that is capable of *transforming* the human spirit and the world that this spirit has created around itself.

To attain this end, it is not sufficient to convince our intellect of a formulation that we define as "truth": it is necessary to work directly on the inner center of all our powers, in order to awaken it to a full consciousness of reality. But this awakening can only be brought about by a change in the direction of our attention. For this we must turn our minds inward to the source of all inspiration, and for this we need certain meditation practices and a ritual preparation such as the practice of *pūjā*, which is itself a kind of dramatized meditation, serving to lead abstract thought beyond its bounds by means of intuitive vision and direct experience, which take its place. For it is only vision and experience that have the power to transform us. Our models and guides are therefore the enlightened ones of past, present, and future who occupy the center of our interest, but not organizations or power and glory, and least of all the number of adherents to our organization or the effectiveness of some propaganda.

We have in the past never tried, and we shall not try in future, to increase the numbers of those world improvers and propagandists who put themselves forward as teachers and gurus by promising their supporters heaven and earth and claiming to teach them easy paths to salvation. We know that we can only free ourselves by hard work on ourselves, and then help others. It is only through an insight that shakes up the depths of our whole personality that we can experience that transforming power that will free us from suffering. But no one can gain this insight except by going on the path that leads to just this insight—gained through inner experience. If we have once experienced this breakthrough, it will thenceforth be our highest task as human beings to show this way to others by our own example, and to fill them with hope and inspiration.

But by thus helping others through our example to tread the path, to understand it and experience it, we fulfill our pledge and gain liberation for ourselves. That is the essence of the bodhisattva way. And everyone who treads this path, whether he professes himself a follower of the "small" or the "great" vehicle or whether he has entrusted himself to the diamond way, deserves our veneration and love. For all the great ones of the various schools of thought who have trodden the path of realization are our teachers.

Among the teachers of the Ārya Maitreya Maṇḍala, Buddhists of *all* schools have been represented: our especial thanks goes to our gurus among the Theravādins as well as the Tibetan Gelugpas, Sakyapas, Kargyütpas, and Nyingmapas. They have all developed one or another aspect of the Dharma in particular, and thus passed on to us their deepened understanding of particular aspects of the path of the Enlightened One. But the Occidental culture in which we have our roots has made its contribution to our spiritual development, as well as the Brahmin tradition, and the great sages of the East. To every one of them, on whose shoulders we stand, our gratitude and veneration are due. For no being develops understanding out of nothing. Whatever comes to be develops in dependence on what has gone before. Thus in our minds we continually re-create the world of *saṃsāra* in its dependently originated arising, while at the same time through recognition and penetration of the universally conditioned nature of all becoming we achieve the breakthrough to liberation from greed, hatred, and the delusion of self, that is: *nirvāṇa*.

But this recognition and this knowledge of how we are bound up in greater relationships does not mean that we are addicted to unbridled syncretism. Our path is the path that the Exalted One, the Buddha, has pointed out. The more clearly we come to see this path, the more profound it becomes and the closer to reality, and with every step it makes us happier and freer.

If we want to make the Dharma of the Exalted One take root in the West, we must continually return to essentials, to that which the Buddha wanted to convey to people, without blindly following current trends, but also without committing ourselves too firmly to any of the historical schools. The schools of the past had their justification in their own time and under the conditions of particular social structures. But everything is subject to change, even the forms of presentation of a teaching and the meditative approach. The Ārya Maitreya Maṇḍala affirms the whole Buddhist tradition, which reflects the spectrum of the Dharma in numerous facets—each after its own fashion. Our aim should be at least to have some presentiment of this fullness, and then, as people of our time, to go our own way unfalteringly in the direction pointed out to us by the Buddha.

We call ourselves a Vajrayāna Sangha. The Vajrayāna was the final development of Buddhism on Indian soil, which integrated all previous schools within itself in such a way that it made continually fresh attempts to reform and transform what had been transmitted. And every one of us must in turn carry out this act of integration individually. We have therefore made it a rule for candidates and members of the order first to study the various schools of the Dharma, and, under guidance, to experience for themselves their principal meditative methods. It is only in this way that the individual can find out by experience how different schools of Buddhism have developed specific aspects of the Dharma and thereby contributed to the total development of Buddhism. The individual thus traverses in abridged form this entire development as a human being of the present day, learning how to distinguish the essential from what is dated and conditioned by its time, and thus maturing as a person capable of being of assistance to others on their path.

In this connection I would like to compare Buddhism to a giant tree that is only viable as a whole: you can't want to have the trunk alone, or just the leaves or the flowers or the seed! Roots, trunk, branches, twigs, leaves, flowers, and seed must be experienced as a unity. It is necessary to realize that this tree once came from a seed and grew up and will continue to grow according to its indwelling law. It would be foolish to seek to deny the development of the tree from the seed and its ever richer unfolding. Anyone who tried to fix the development of the tree at a particular stage would deprive it of life. And it would be just as foolish to seek to use only a particular part of the tree in the belief that one had thereby embraced the whole. But that is just what many people do today when they want to make Buddhist propaganda. They see everything only from their own narrow standpoint, and imagine that is the whole.

In our work in the West, we have the great opportunity today presented by a new beginning. We are not bound to any one national tradition of Buddhism, and we do not need to carry around with us the burden of an outmoded inheritance. We can approach Buddhism in the spirit of beginners, and, on account of the liberty that Western science and the freedom-loving development of thought of the last few centuries have given us, we have the chance to observe without prejudice the living dynamism of the development of Buddhism through the thousands of years of its existence. In this way we can gain an overall picture of the variety of forms that developed at an early date in India before spreading to South, Central, and East Asia and unfolding there. Every one of these forms is a grandiose and unique creation that accentuates and displays the different aspects of the Buddha Dharma, so that it is of importance not only for its own time and culture, but also for the further development of the Dharma as a whole.

It is for us now to integrate this rich variety into a whole, without clinging to any one particular tradition. We respect the different traditions as they are, without trying merely to imitate them. For if we were to imitate any one particular tradition, we would be binding ourselves to something that belonged to a different time and a different culture. We would be merely exchanging our own tradition for another—which in the long run would be senseless. And so we do not want to turn our members into little Indians, Tibetans, Japanese, or Chinese, but rather to attempt first of all to understand the true nature of our own Western tradition and culture in its full development,* and then on that basis to study the traditions of other cultures and to have an understanding respect for them.

We live in a world today that is being drawn closer and closer together. Western technology and science are reaching all the nations of the East—not always to their advantage. Eastern wisdom—often misunderstood—is flooding westward, offering Western people a counterbalance of calm and contemplation in the midst of their continual unrest. Thus we are on the way toward one world. It is to be hoped that the next centuries will increasingly further this process of fusion, so that all people will feel themselves to be citizens of this one world, not merely as members of a particular nation or race. It will be the task of the Buddhist Sangha—as we understand it—to play a part in this work of global integration. But to be able to fulfill this mission, the Sangha must continually redefine its own position in a changing world, just as has always happened in the twenty-five-hundred-year-old history of Buddhism and through which the dynamism of the Dharma has manifested at all times.

During the Buddha's lifetime the Sangha consisted of the *caturvargas*, the "four communities" of *bhikṣus, bhikṣunīs, upāsakas* and *upāsikās,*† who were all considered "noble disciples of the

---

*The study of the history of Western culture shows clearly that it cannot be described as a purely "Christian" culture. Rather, Christianity in spreading throughout Europe was partly formed and conditioned by both the pre-Christian cultures of the West and the advent of Islam, factors that affected it both positively and negatively.

†*Bhikṣus* (Pali *bhikkhus*) and *bhikṣunīs* (P. *bhikkhunīs*), that is, "mendicants," are the fully ordained members of the monastic Sangha, who at their ordination *(upasampadā)* have taken on some 250 rules of the order (those for nuns are stricter and more numerous). The Order also includes male and female novices (Skt. *śrāmaṇera/ī,* Pali *sāmaṇero/ī*), who at the "going forth" ceremony (Skt. *pravrajyā,* Pali *pabbajjā*) have undertaken the ten *śīlas*. The *upāsakas* and *upāsikās* ("sitting near," because the Buddha, when he gave instruction after a meal in the home of lay followers, let the host and hostess sit beside him) are disciples who have remained in the household life, and have undertaken the five *śīlas*. The term "layman" or "lay follower" is wrong, because from the very

Exalted One"; those of them who lived in the world (the *upāsakas* and *upāsikās*) were just as capable of attaining to the lofty goal—the Deathless—as the *bhikṣus* and *bhikṣunis* in the order, and did so (see *Anguttara Nikāya* 1.14 [*Kindred Sayings* i.22ff.]). At this early period of Buddhism, the monastic Sangha had the particular function of preserving and spreading the teaching. At a time when books were unknown or, later, were the privileged possession of the few who were literate, the continued existence of the Dharma depended entirely on the activity of the monastic community, whose task it was to retain the sacred word of memory from generation to generation, and to pass it on. As preservers of the Word of the Buddha, the Sangha gained the upper hand, and the *upāsakas* and *upāsikās* living the household life were degraded to the status of mere almsgivers.

One the other hand, members of the Sangha were thus provided with an opportunity to lead a life free from worldly cares, in order the better to serve the community of disciples who lived in the world. However, instead of this, some cut themselves off in certain orthodox circles; in fact, certain *sūtras* that dealt with meditative and psychological subjects were recited only among the monks, so that the Buddha's principle of "not holding anything back in a closed fist" was abandoned.

The threat of petrifaction and degeneration was countered by those unknown men and women who elevated the bodhisattva ideal to the status of a new guiding principle within Buddhism. This involved a conscious turning away from the purely monastic lifestyle of the previous centuries, and at the same time a renewal of the links between human beings by the reestablishment of the equality of monks and disciples "living in the world," which found its expression in the *Ārya Vimalakīrti-Nirdeśa Nāma Mahāyāna-*

---

beginning there were highly learned *upāsakas* and *upāsikās*, skilled in meditation *(paṇḍitas)*, and, on the other hand, there were also uneducated monks.

It is in these four groups that we find the *ārya-śrāvakas* (Pali *ariya-sāvakas*), the "noble disciples" who are treading the higher path *(pratipadā*, Pali *paṭipadā)*. But not every *bhikṣu* or *upāsaka* is an *ārya-śrāvaka* (the same as Pali *ariya puggala*). He becomes this only when he has attained to "stream-entry" (Pali *sotāpatti*) as a fully committed follower of the Noble Path. Otherwise—whether *bhikṣu* or *upāsaka*—he remains a *pṛthagjana* (Pali *puthujjana*) or "worldling," that is, a being who neither has been liberated from the fetters of greed, hatred, and delusion nor is on the way to liberating himself from these bonds (*Puggala Paññatti* 1.9).

Sūtram (English version by Sara Boin from the French translation of Etienne Lamotte, London: Pali Text Society, 1976). The decisive point was no longer a person's status as monk or layperson, but solely that person's degree of realization on the path to enlightenment. And when, in the following centuries, an exaggerated scholasticism systematized intellectually the meditative experiences of previous generations and became so intoxicated with theory as to put spontaneous meditative experience in the background, the dynamism of the Dharma revealed itself yet again in the paradoxical dialectics of the *Prajñāpāramitā Sūtras* and the shock therapy of Nāgārjuna's transcending of thought in the Mādhyamaka. This led to a return to the meditative roots of Buddhism, resulting in the emergence of the meditation schools, the early Pure Land, and the early Mantrayāna and Vajrayāna. Through the meeting of Buddhism and Taoism, Ch'an arose, which later, in Japan, became linked with the warrior spirit of the Samurai and sublimated the latter in the form of Zen.

When, in India, the Vajrayāna also threatened to become set after its first creative phase, and formalistic moralism became rampant, the *siddhas* brought a fresh dynamism into the Buddhist Dharma, which retained its impetus up to the eleventh century and powerfully influenced the Buddhism of Tibet. And when, from about the fifteenth century, Buddhism began to petrify in practically all Asian countries, with a fixation on the past and its attitudes, accompanied by a partial degeneration of meditation into a series of formal acts and procedures, again new moves toward a fresh start began to show themselves in the past century. In connection with these the role of the Theosophical movement—whatever else one may think of it—must be stressed. This movement not only inspired the Buddhists of Asia with courage, it also contributed greatly to making the Dharma known in the West. And that provided Buddhism with its great chance of a new development in a form adequate to the present time—at whose beginnings we now find ourselves.

In our present time, when the teachings of the Enlightened One are available to all who wish to know through books, and in which a certain degree of general education makes it possible to understand these texts, a Buddhist Sangha must no longer be based on a community of monks and nuns supported by the community, but should in the first place demonstrate the realization of the Buddhist teaching is also possible *in the midst of daily life*.

Thus the Sangha today should not represent an exceptional condition of human existence, but must become a preparer of the way, concerned with the spreading of methods for the practical realization of the Dharma so as to be available to all and in conformity with conditions of life in our time. Accordingly, the concept of the Sangha can no longer be equated with monasticism, but must be established on the ideal of the Buddhist way of life, which shall lead all people to a new form of life embracing all human functions and capabilities. We should also learn the lesson of history, that the overemphasis on the monastic Sangha, combined with neglect or depreciation of the *upāsakas*, has repeatedly brought Buddhism into a situation whereby in certain countries in which it had previously flourished it was possible for it to be almost entirely destroyed, once the monastic Sangha had been exterminated.

The mere fact that the Buddha, right down to his final human existence, led a full life in the world, with wife and child, and still attained enlightenment in that same life should teach us all not to obstruct our path through the enforced repression of normal human functions and capabilities. It is only through the fullness of experience and the living of a *full* human existence that we can attain to that turning within and transformation that alone can lead to the spontaneous experience of enlightenment.

But here the question poses itself: how can we maintain the spontaneity of spirit, the vigor, lack of prejudice, and receptivity of our minds—or, to put it another way, the "beginner's mind" that should be the mark of the Buddhist? Assuredly not in the safe haven and unworried life of the monastery, where one is drawn into a highly organized, unproblematic way of life that sinks to a mere customary routine if it becomes a permanent state.

The order founded by the Buddha was a community of seekers after truth, who as wandering monks (*parivrājaka*, Pali *paribbājaka*) with no house or home traveled about the country, unencumbered by possessions, and in continual contact with people with whose needs and problems they sympathized without themselves becoming involved. The Buddha addressed to them the famous words of the *Mahāvagga* of the Vinaya Piṭaka (*Book of Discipline*): "Go forth, monks, and wander for the gain of many, for the welfare of many, out of compassion for the world, for the good, the gain, the welfare of gods and men. . . . proclaim, monks, a consummate, perfect and pure life of holiness." And in the repeated description of the ideal wandering monk he says: "Full of sympathy, he has love and compassion for all beings." And the way of pilgrimage is described, in contrast to the "prison of domesticity," as "the free open air." It was only when the Order had become a regulated institution with fixed dwellings in the form of extensive monasteries that the necessity arose for a moral code covering all possible details. Just before his death, the Buddha made a final attempt to free the Order from the embrace of these rules that suppressed all spontaneity and all living intuition. Recalling the times when these rules neither existed nor were necessary, in which a simple "Come!" (*Ehi bhikkhu!*) sufficed for acceptance into the company of disciples, the Buddha offered the community the opportunity to return to the simplicity of the early days, or at least to shed a good part of the ballast that had been accumulated like an incrustation in the course of the years. He said: "If they wish, the order may alter the minor rules after my passing." ("Ākaṅkhamāno Ānanda saṃgho mam' accayena khuddânukhuddakāni sikkhāpadāni samūhantu," *Mahāparinibbāna Sutta, Dīgha Nikāya* 16.6.3).

In this connection we might also mention a story told in the *Vinaya* about a monk who declared that he wanted to leave the Order because he was in despair about all the many rules of *vinaya*. The Buddha asked him if he could keep just three rules. When the monk agreed to this, the Buddha said, "The first rule is, keep your body under control. The second is, keep your speech under control. The third is, keep your mind under control." These three rules include the entire *vinaya*, which is binding on every Buddhist.

When the Buddha, shortly before his passing, directed the words quoted above to the monks, the elders among them, who had grown fixed in their ways, were silent, believing that not even the Buddha could teach them any more. And so the great opportunity was missed, and it took almost another five hundred years before the living spirit once more burst forth out of the petrified tradition and the followers of the Enlightened One recognized the *ideal of Buddhahood* as the only goal worth striving for by the noblest of mankind.

When, after another five hundred years, this ideal too began to be strangled by scholastic learning, the most serious seekers after truth once more went forth into homelessness outside of monasteries and religious institutions, and discovered that enlightenment could be gained, not only through monasticism in the security of the monastery, but above all in the readiness to take on human existence with all its suffering and inadequacies and to transform it by converting the transient elements of existence into organs of a higher, universal wisdom. In this way the elements (Skt. *skandha*) of the human personality become vehicles of liberation, in fact the very same five *skandhas* that bind the unenlightened to *saṃsāra* serve the one on the road to enlightenment as a means to the realization of the highest goal. In the enlightened person they finally become qualities of Buddhahood, as they are experienced and represented in meditative vision in the form of the Dhyāni Buddhas.

In other words, the principles of corporeality, sensations or feelings, perception, willing and the formative powers, and consciousness are transformed by the event of enlightenment into qualities corresponding to the nature of a Buddha. These qualities have no ego reference and are thus no longer limited by the concept of an ego, but are all-embracing, that is, in the truest sense universal. Thus the entire universe becomes the "body" of the Enlightened One, his feelings become the expression of all-embracing compassion, his perception the clarity of vision of the distinguishing wisdom, his will the selfless volition of the all-accomplishing deed, and his consciousness the universal enlightenment-consciousness.

From this vantage point, the concept of the Sangha is expanded from that of a mere monastic community (or even of a community of those on the way to enlightenment) to a community of the enlightened, the holy ones, those who have become "whole" in past, present, and future. This is expressed in the Tibetan tradition, as for instance in the *mKhas Grub rjes* ("Fundamentals of the Tibetan Tantras"), where we find this verse:

> I venerate the Sangha of those
> who, having gained liberation,
> teach the Path of Liberation,
> who, well-established in the holy life,
> possess the good qualities of the sacred realm.

Thus, when we take refuge in the Sangha, we take refuge in the community of the enlightened and of all those who have realized liberation.

But if we speak of the Sangha as a community of those striving for enlightenment, that is, of those treading the path of bodhisattvahood, then all belong to the Sangha who have dedicated their life and thought to the enlightened ones and, in the experience of the initiatory consecration, have taken them into their own deepest consciousness, in order by meditative vision to make them an active force in their lives and thus one making for realization. Such a Sangha as this does not necessarily call for monks or nuns (though it does not exclude these); it is a community of the spirit and of the inner path whereby the wholeness and perfection of man is realized. It is the path of spontaneous experience and intuition arising from an openness to the holy and the elevated.

However, at this point it is necessary to point out a danger that can arise if someone, without guidance or with wrong guidance, follows his spontaneous ideas, which he calls "intuitions." After all, how can we know whether what we regard as "intuition" is right or wrong? It is good to have intuitions, but we must secure them with the aid of clear thinking and understanding. Only then can we, in the course of time, develop a feeling that tells us whether our intuition corresponds to reality. For if one has had a vague feeling or an "intuition" that cannot be verified as to its reality or in the realm of human experience, then one has probably merely had a waking dream. But if our intuition is not actually contrary to the facts of life, then we can at least assume that it may be of some use to us. If we act otherwise, we split the world up into two separate spheres of experience that are in conflict with each other and thus lead people into schizoid states.

There are today various philosophical, religious, and mystical systems that neglect thinking and concentrate their whole attention on "intuition" or "inspiration." These groups are in a certain sense a necessary counterbalance to the excessive intellectuality of our present-day culture. But these people have fallen from one extreme into another. Buddhism is the middle way that passes between the extremes and at the same times moves beyond them.

For this reason, it is best to start by gaining a basic knowledge of the three *yānas* or vehicles of Buddhism (Hīnayāna, Mahāyāna, and Vajrayāna). In this way, three different dimensions of the human spirit are assimilated. The first is principally based on thought, the second, together with a sympathetic direction of mind towards all beings, is based on a dialectic philosophy, while the third provides a practice leading to the experience itself. Philosophy without such a practice is senseless and useless, because everything then remains as it was. But the reverse way also leads to nothing. If we follow a practice, such as a method of meditation, for which one is not spiritually prepared and which therefore one does not understand, the powers activated by the practice are dispersed. It is therefore necessary for us on the one hand to develop a clear view of the facts of life, and then, in addition, to strive to develop a continually renewed integrating vision against the background of an "experienceable transcendence" that gives a direction to our practice.

Anyone setting out on the path of freedom must first of all recognize what it is that binds and enslaves him and what can make liberation possible. In order to gain this insight, we need to conduct an unprejudiced examination of the world that surrounds us. Through this we learn to realize that our life is not restricted to the narrow circle of our immediate surroundings, but is a part of the universe whose boundaries we cannot know and in which we are held by a network of innumerable mutually conditioned factors. Only one who has gained this insight as a real experience can begin the task of working on oneself, and at the beginning there is a voluntarily accepted ordering of one's actions, as is reflected, for instance, in the *śīlas*, or in the steps of the Noble Eightfold Path. This leads to a harmony between person and surroundings, thereby creating an indispensable precondition for progress on the spiritual path.

This progress on the path of Dharma is characterized by a profound transformation in the human personality in the form of a heroic commitment of all one's psychic energy (*vīrya*, Pali *viriya*). The conditions for such a fundamental restructuring of an individual are, first, the freedom of human decision and will, and second, the factor of impermanence inherent in all created things (*anitya*, Pali *anicca*), and thus the possibility of change.

In his discourses the Buddha repeatedly stressed that all things in this world are subject to constant change. He showed that whatever has come into existence cannot possibly endure. But this in itself neutral statement of the Buddha's was soon taken to mean that change and alteration is in itself an evil, and that transience, as the word *anitya/anicca* was interpreted, was a *negative* feature applying to all things. And since everything in this world is subject to the great law of change and disappearance, life in the here and now was negated and a "state" of permanence in a realm "where there is neither coming nor going" was conceived (*Udāna* 8.2).

Such a limited idea, however, which is wholly opposed to the *anātman* experience, conflicts with the teaching of the Buddha, which tells us that a human birth in this world is the best possible kind of birth—the great opportunity that opens up for us the way to liberation. Human existence, according to Buddhism, offers the most favorable and fortunate starting point, since it provides us with freedom of choice and decision. None of the other worlds open to us, however pleasant they may be—such as the world of *devas* (gods or glorified spirits, lit. "shining ones")—can offer us the same great possibilities for development that our human state provides. The doctrine of the six realms of existence that we meet again and again in the canonical texts tries to impress this on us ever afresh, in order to make it very clear to the hearer or reader what he is missing if he does not act here and now.

Thus, for instance, we are shown how a being in the animal kingdom has no choice, it must follow its instincts. And if a being is born, as a result of good karma, among the gods, it at first enjoys pure happiness. But since the experience of suffering is not continually present to its consciousness, such a being has difficulty in recognizing the world of reality before, "at the expiry of its good karma," experiencing suffering at the time of fading away from there. Such a being will all too easily miss the chance of entering on the path of enlightenment.

During the first centuries after the passing of the Buddha, a strongly ascetic attitude was predominant in the monastic Sangha, propagating a flight from the world: by avoiding all contact with normal life one could avoid suffering, since the forms of life were all recognized as transient and full of suffering.

This extreme form of pessimism called forth a reaction in the Sangha, which began to gain strength about three centuries after the *parinirvāṇa* of the Buddha. With an appeal to the Dharma as represented by the Buddha's own life, the principle was evolved that one should not flee from suffering but willingly accept it in order to be led to purification thereby. This was that great movement that became known under the name of Mahāyāna, according to which enlightenment was the only worthy aim of a follower of the Buddha. But this aim was only possible by following the Buddha on the bodhisattva path, whereby one identified with all suffering beings and thus took upon oneself the sufferings of the world. In this way the entire world was drawn into the process of liberation, and the suffering was overcome by a compassion that was so all-embracing that all personal sorrow lost its meaning, so that one forgot one's own suffering over that of other beings. For as long as we are trapped in egocentricity, thinking only of our own happiness and rejecting all suffering, we are feeding our ego and thus blocking our own path to a breakthrough. But if we accept our own experience of suffering and allow it to ripen into compassion in the act of identification with all suffering beings, we transform this suffering into a means of liberation, a purifying power that speeds the process of spiritual awakening.

In the first century B.C.E. the Mahāyāna movement gained supporters in the Indian subcontinent, replacing the monastic ideal of striving for one's own enlightenment by the ideal of bodhisattvahood. And with the development of the Mahāyāna the step was undertaken from the idea of individual liberation from a world of misery and transience to the recognition that the change and decay of everything that has come to be in this world also means the *transformability* of the world. Starting from the solidarity of all beings at the highest level of our consciousness, the Four Divine Abidings (*brahmavihāras:* love, compassion, sympathetic joy, and equanimity toward whatever happens to oneself) were raised to the highest virtues of human existence, which lead to liberation from all self-attachment and egocentricity.

With the arising and development of the last great school of Buddhism in its homeland of India, the Vajrayāna (second to tenth century C.E.), the work of meditation (its conditions, its possibilities, and its practice in daily life) was put right in the forefront of religious life, and everything else was subordinated or related to it. The philosophical and psychological hypotheses for this new school were taken from the Mādhyamaka philosophy of Nāgārjuna, and still more from the Vijñānavāda and Yogācāra system of Maitreyanātha, Asaṅga, and Vasubandhu, in addition to the later works of the great *siddhas* of the sixth to eighth centuries.

Starting from a dynamic synthesis of the already existing philosophical schools of Buddhism, which it integrated into itself, the Vajrayāna worked out the psychological consequences of the potential universality of the individual consciousness, going further and stressing that *every* aspect of the human personality could be transformed into a means of liberation—even those aspects that at first seem to us like hindrances on the path. In this way it taught us how we can so transform our life that our entire thinking, feeling, speech, and action becomes increasingly an expression of the fundamental unity of *saṃsāra* and *nirvāṇa*, that is, of the interrelationship of physical and psychical qualities, of the sensual and the transcendental, of the individual and the universal. And so we proceed from the recognition of the transformability of the world (or from the knowledge of the relativity of *saṃsāra* and *nirvāṇa* as the two aspects of the same reality, which only exist in their mutual conditionality), to a practical method of transformation, in which all the psychic factors of a human being, and above all the unlimited potentialities of that being's depth-consciousness are drawn in together, so that the individual becomes aware of its universality and can realize itself in its totality.

Thus the development of Buddhism on Indian soil displays three dimensions of the spirit, in such a way that each succeeding dimension does not deny the preceding one, but includes its qualities and integrates them at a more comprehensive level or into a network of more extensive relations. Thus the ethical principles (*śīla*) of early Buddhism together with the Four Noble Truths (*catvāri-ārya-satyāni*, Pali *cattāri ariya-saccāni*) are the foundation on which the Mahāyāna built up its high philosophy of Śūnyavāda, Vijñānavāda, and so on, while the Vajrayāna is the application of the Mahāyāna philosophy (*prajñā*), which, together with the discipline of early Buddhism, is elevated to the principle of inner transformation and unification (*samādhi*) through particular systems of meditation and yogic practice.

The three basic principles of the Noble Eightfold Path that leads to liberation (*śīla, samādhi, prajñā*, Pali *sīla, samādhi, paññā*) can therefore be regarded as the distinguishing marks of the *yānas:* all three principles are contained in each of the three vehicles, but the emphasis varies according to the inner attitude of each school. Over the centuries that led to varying interpretations and evaluations, in the course of which some traditional concepts were given a new meaning. While the essential teachings of the Exalted One were retained, the forms of doctrine and meditation were developed in accordance with the changing social structure of the first post-Buddhist millennium. Whereas early Buddhism was realistic and analytic, the Mahāyāna, particularly under the influence of Nāgārjuna and his pupils, developed an idealist-monistic conception, which was then developed in the Vajrayāna through creative imagery and inner vision to a new method through which the total human personality experienced a transformation and unification.

Early Buddhism teaches us to see the world *yathā bhūtaṃ*, "just as it is," without asking whether this world is real or not. In the

Mahāyāna the character of "objective" reality is denied for the world, being replaced by an abstract transcendent reality bare of all qualities and attributes, which can only be paraphrased as *śūnyatā* or "emptiness." But this emptiness is at the same time infinite potentiality, which the Vajrayāna recognizes as the primal quality of consciousness and itself regards as the final instance of all understanding and all creative reality, beyond which it is impossible for either thought or experience to go. Even the enlightenment of an Awakened One is a phenomenon of consciousness.

It necessarily follows that reality is not an abstract "being thus" or a rigid "absolute" principle, but the dynamic working of consciousness as a living force that brings forth and embraces everything. To the extent that the individual consciousness becomes aware of its potential and original universality, its experience of reality becomes intensified, as does its cosmogonic power of creative participation, world transformation, integrative fusion and realization of wholeness. Through this, the body as microcosm becomes an image of the universe, a temple of transformation, in which all the higher powers wait to be awakened. The body becomes the great *maṇḍala*, the "magic circle" in which the great transformation takes place. Thus, the path has led from suffering because of impermanence, through compassion with all beings to the acceptance of suffering as a means of purification and liberation from all the bonds of selfhood.

We realize that many Buddhist schools adopt and develop other points of view. We have no wish for a confrontation between our standpoint and that of other Buddhist schools. Every path is a practicable path as soon as we tread it. But whoever continually changes methods and schools will never reach the goal. Buddhism was always concerned to respect other faiths and other people's opinions, ready to understand others while calmly proceeding on its own way. Only so was it possible in ancient India for the followers of all sorts of Buddhist schools to live together in the same monastery and argue together without the one condemning the other's point of view, as so often happens in the confrontations within monotheistic religions.

We Buddhists in the West must learn from the historical schools of the East until—without changing the essential content of the teaching—we have found the mode of expression, and the path, that suits us. Doctrinal concepts in Buddhism have always only had the significance of a finger pointing out the way—a way that must be *trodden*. And, just as hitherto each country has made a valuable contribution to the development of Buddhism, so now we too in the West, if the doctrine of the Enlightened One is to take root here, must make our own contribution to its further unfolding, and fill it with fresh lifeblood.

The Dharma of the Buddha is not a religion based on belief. Its basis is our own uninterrupted work on ourselves, and this will lead us to its sources, which are meditative experience and understanding. Therefore, Buddhism is a religion that has to be reborn afresh in every individual being. But in order not to endanger the meditative experience through ready-made suggestions, thus blocking spontaneous experience and discovery in advance, we must free ourselves from the tyranny of traditionally inherited concepts (which can too easily solidify to narrow dogmas). Concepts—as abstractions from what has been or can be experienced—have a life of their own and become changed in the course of centuries, thus often in later times being far removed from the original basic experience that gave them birth. Accordingly, concepts can only be equated, in principle, within the narrow framework of a particular culture at a particular time.

At the same time we must also be on our guard against making the other error so common today, based on the similarity of certain formulations in Buddhism and in the writings of certain European thinkers and mystics, or modern existentialists, scientists, and psychologists, of falling into the trap of assuming that "it's all the same"; this leveling process, which in a pseudoscientific way believes in everything and nothing, leads then to a confused kind of syncretism that is finally declared to be "religious tolerance" and even "the essence of all religiosity."

Of course one can respect any spiritual form of expression, whether one shares it or not, as a product of life in all its variety, in the same way as in a garden we admire the variety of plants without making our own preferences a standard of judgment. The essential point is to maintain that ever watchful and open receptivity of mind that does not exclude any manifestation, but that remains capable of distinguishing whatever is genuine from the artificially constructed. In this way we will be in a position to proceed undistractedly on our own path, and to understand the paths of others without imitating them.

There is absolutely no need to know all the ways and forms of expression of the spiritual life. A wise man is not one who knows a lot, but one who is always ready to extend his knowledge when he comes into contact with what he does not know. Ignorance consists of a mind that closes up and blocks itself off, not being willing to learn anything new, irrespective of whether it has piled up a great deal of factual knowledge or not. Wisdom, on the other hand, is the sign of an open mind, and nirvāṇa—freedom from greed, hatred, and delusion—is at the same time freedom from all prejudices, because greed, as a blind desiring, hatred as a blind rejection, and delusion as the egocentricity that wraps everything in darkness, all prevent the full opening of the mind and receptivity for whatever life has to offer.

And so the Ārya Maitreya Maṇḍala is not meant as a refuge for narrowminded dogmatists or weary aesthetes; rather, it aims to serve the present and future of Buddhism, which we have to continually re-create through our ever watchful, active communal efforts. For however much we may admire the great achievements of the past, we do not believe we can be satisfied with what was gained once or long ago. We must continue building on the foundations of the past, without exhausting ourselves in continual repetition. Just as past generations in different cultures gave Buddhism a continually new face, we too must work at the Buddhism of our time and culture in order to bring it close to the people of our time, who are in need of it.

We pay our profoundest respects to the forms created in previous ages, and we know that we can learn from them. But we would hinder our own growth and condemn Buddhism to death if we were to remain bound to the old forms. Life knows no standing still, and whatever does not grow must die. Therefore we want to profit from the experiences of the past, without clinging to them, by using them as our starting point as we build for the future, making the essential features of *all* Buddhist schools our basis.

Thus, we commit ourselves to the discipline of early Buddhism, to the world-acceptance and social orientation of the Mahāyāna, to the great discoveries of Nāgārjuna, Asaṅga, and Vasubandhu, to the psychology of the Vajrayāna, the mysticism of the Nyingmapas, the historical sense of the Sakyapas, the meditational experiences of the early Kargyütpas, the systematism of the Gelugpas, the breakthrough of the intellect in Ch'an and Zen, as well as the deep faith of the followers of Amitābha. It is in the inclusion of all these historically developed forms, which all developed from the central idea of Buddhism, that we see the basis for the *further development* of Buddhism in our own time.

We therefore welcome and assent to the efforts of various Tibetan, Japanese, Sinhalese, Thai, and other Buddhist scholars who are spreading the ideas of their schools in the West. They will all find people who are ready to tread their path. The Dharma embraces many paths, and whoever has understood it neither feels any ambition to collect many pupils around him nor imagines that he alone has the true interpretation and the only proper method of meditation.

In fact, the Dharma of the Buddha differs from many other forms of religion in that it does not demand of its followers that they should believe in anything that lies beyond the experience of the individual. It allows a fresh view of reality to ripen within us, which grows from an experience that is only possible through hard work on ourselves and service to others. The resultant vision of reality, undistorted by any flaws or prejudices, is called the "state of mind connected with the knowledge of the great mirror" (*mahād-arśa-jñāna-samprayukta-citta-varga*). From this there develops, in the course of further meditative work, the knowledge of nondifference and essential identity of all that lives, and there develops within us the "state of mind connected with the knowledge of equality" (*samatā-jñāna-samprayukta-citta-varga*), which awakens in us the feeling of solidarity with all that lives, and permits us to accept and respect, through the vision of their common origin, the individual differences of beings as a unique manifestation of the whole, resulting in consequence of their karmic development.

This wisdom arises in us at the third stage of meditative insight through the distinguishing and discerning wisdom of Amitābha *(pratyavekṣaṇajñāna)*. The attitude it produces, in which similarity of origin and difference of individual development (and thus of formation) are perceived as a whole, forms the basis of our order. Thus the great demand made in early Buddhism in the Pali canon, to liken others to oneself (*attānaṃ upamaṃ katvā, Dhammapada* 129, 130), directs the Buddha's disciple onto the path of bodhisattvahood, in order to awaken in him the *bodhicitta*—the thought of enlightenment. But once this has awakened in him, his whole life becomes transformed. With the untiring application of all his energies he will work at himself in order to be able more and more perfectly to labor for the good of all living beings. His perfection will be attained in the karma-free deed that brings everything to perfection (*kṛtyānuṣṭhāna-jñāna-samprayukta-citta-varga*), which for the Buddhist is embodied in the great bodhisattvas, and which in our community is symbolically expressed in the figure of Ārya Maitreya.

The tremendous changes that this noble figure of Ārya Maitreya has produced in the development of Buddhism over thousands of years are a proof of its life and capacity for development. Its effect is felt today far beyond the boundaries of traditional Buddhism. That which twenty-five hundred years ago was a symbol of the distant future, being overshadowed by the presence on earth of a still active Enlightened One, took on ever more concrete form within a very few centuries after the *parinirvāṇa* of Śākyamuni Buddha, and has today become the living hope of millions of spiritually aware people all over the world, and especially of those who, having broken away from old established forms and traditions of faith, are looking for new and more realistic values. For today, for the first time, there is awakening in mankind the consciousness of planetary unity that embraces us all in one fate, and that brings the individual into a deeper relationship with the whole.

From this consciousness that shattered the foundations of our being there arose anew the spiritual solidarity, which first found its symbolic expression in Maitreya, the bodhisattva filled with love, and which finally led to the rebirth of Buddhism on the all-inclusive path of bodhisattvahood.

Just as today a tremendous revolution is taking place, arising from the growing recognition of common humanity and bursting the narrow frontiers of nations, races, religions, and cultures, so too the bodhisattva ideal burst the boundaries of a monastically oriented Buddhism seeking to escape the world. It changed it from a collection of schools, each of which claimed to possess the true interpretation of the Buddha's teaching, into a world religion in which the salvation of the individual takes second place to the self-sacrificing task of working for the salvation of all beings, and in which fellow-feeling with all that lives triumphs over escape from one's own suffering.

This complete turn in spiritual attitude toward the problem of suffering is nowhere made so clear as in the readiness, expressed in the bodhisattva vow, rather to take upon oneself the suffering of the entire world than to turn one's back on the world for the sake of one's own salvation. That this decisive turning toward others should actually be the first step toward the overcoming of suffering, and therefore to enlightenment, may at first seem paradoxical; the solution lies in the fact that the turning toward others makes the hardened ego-structure transparent. In the same measure as the inner development proceeds, the individual's feeling of responsibility grows and finally ripens to a universal responsibility that, with a properly focused commitment of all one's forces, aims at nothing less than the perfect enlightenment of a buddha for the benefit and welfare of all beings.

It is always said that a bodhisattva-mahāsattva rejects entry into "final" *nirvāṇa* (Skt. *parinirvāṇa*) in order to help all beings. But we could only speak of such a "rejection" by the bodhisattva if *nirvāṇa* were to be interpreted in the sense of a quietist ideal state of individual liberation from suffering. If, however, we remain within the realm of the Buddha's own definition of the word, as "the cessation of greed, hatred, and delusion" (which has nothing to do with metaphysical speculation or with a state of quietist yearning), there can be no question of any "rejection of *nirvāṇa*." That would be nothing but the intentional retention of the very ignorance from which the three negative qualities arise again and again.

However, as a wisdom being, the bodhisattva certainly does not reject complete understanding. On the contrary, for the sake of perfect enlightenment he rejects any *purely personal* delivery from suffering, just as the Buddha of our age did, and all the Enlightened Ones of past ages, in order to let all their fellow beings share in their own enlightenment and to light in them the spark of enlightenment-consciousness *(bodhicitta)*. As Har Dayal remarks in his book *The Bodhisattva Doctrine in Buddhist Sanskrit Literature* (London, 1932), the Buddha did not use the word *nibbāna* at all in his first sermon (if we follow the oldest written records), but instead referred to "the highest perfect enlightenment" (Pali *anuttara sammāsambodhi*). But this is the goal toward which everyone who is a follower of the Buddha should strive, without caring whether he gains this goal in this or some other life. In fact, even if this goal were unattainable (and the existence of the historical Buddha and his enlightened predecessors are the surest guarantee that this is not the case), this would necessarily shine forth as a glorious light by which to guide our lives.

In the bodhisattva Maitreya this guiding image takes shape, for he is, like us, one who is still in the process of becoming, and present. And as we grow, or rather inwardly grow together with him, he becomes the image of our own depth-consciousness. Every one of the buddhas of the past was, according to the general Buddhist idea, on the one hand the incorporation of that universal consciousness that is common to all enlightened beings, and on the other hand he was the highest form of expression of the spirit of the age in a particular epoch of world history and human history. For instance, in the magic age that preceded the awakening of the intellect, Kassapa Buddha was distinguished by his magic powers. Gautama Śākyamuni Buddha, on the other hand, the fourth buddha of our epoch, represented the energy of clear thought: the formulation of dependent origination in its causal, conditional, and simultaneously synchronic connection was the greatest act of creative thought of his time. In addition, he represented the will-dominated goal orientation (*vīrya*, Pali *viriya*).

Maitreya, the coming buddha, will follow the age of intellectual achievements by bringing in an expanded and intensified intuitive consciousness, in which the feeling of the essential unity of all life will help an active love of one's fellow beings to emerge. But this active love, which has nothing in common with the sentimental-emotional attitude of ecstatic and pietistic sects, is the practical working out and application of Amitābha's discriminating wisdom (*pratyavekṣana-jñāna*), in which the warmth of feeling combines with the clarity of inner vision, and finds its expression in the selfless (and therefore karma-free) action of Amoghasiddhi. But Maitreya is the embodiment of Amoghasiddhi's all-embracing wisdom, that is, the spontaneous, selfless loving act that does not bind the doer but makes him happy and free, because his action flows from devotion and not self-reference.

This readiness to act is indicated in many representations of Maitreya as sitting in "European" style, that is, with both feet on the ground—not sunk in meditation, but ready to stand up in order to bring consolation and help to suffering humanity. While his right hand is raised to the level of the heart in a gesture of teaching and blessing, his left hand, which rests in his lap, holds a vessel with the elixir of immortality *(amṛta-kalaśa)*, which links him with Amitāyus and Avalokiteśvara, whose function he takes over in his earthly career. In Japan the statues of Miroku (Maitreya) and Kwannon (Avalokiteśvara) are often shown in the same posture: left foot on the ground, the right foot on the left knee—thus bringing out clearly the similarity of their function and character. The link with Śākyamuni, whose successor on earth Maitreya is, is indicated by a small *stūpa*, which is often seen above the brow in the front part of Maitreya's hair. According to legend, the future Śākyamuni Buddha before his descent from the Tuṣita heaven gave his bodhisattva crown to Maitreya, thus appointing him as his successor: the buddha of the next and last epoch of this world age.

With the turning to Maitreya the ever-growing consciousness of present and future reveals itself, which is not satisfied with looking back to the past, but recognizes the creative present as the most important aspect of time because it is the only one that is capable of realization and that forms the future, and in which what is past—fused into present-day life and awakened to new existence—is poured into fresh molds and so transformed.

It was this fundamental conception that led the first patriarch of the Ārya Maitreya Maṇḍala Order, the Most Venerable Tomo Geshe Rinpoche Ngawang Kalzang, to proclaim his vision of a Buddhism oriented on the future in Tibet and India. He gave this change of direction away from the previously almost exclusive preoccupation with the past symbolic expression by making Maitreya the central image of a movement for spiritual renewal. Ārya Maitreya was proclaimed by him as a bond linking all Buddhist schools through the hope of the continuity of enlightened world-teachers. In Maitreya he saw the almost living embodiment of the bodhisattva ideal in its self-sacrificing humanity.

At the same time, he also saw Maitreya as a bridge that over and above all differences should join the *essence* of all traditions of the Buddhist Dharma with the present and future. In other words, this figure represented for him the living dynamism of Buddhism, which—without reducing or calling into question the values and significance of previous stages—takes seriously the idea of nonattachment to what is past, which underlies the Buddhist Dharma. In this way all persons striving after a breakthrough would become free to lead a conscious life in the present. With his gaze fixed on the future, man will be able, in a continually changing process of development, to act selflessly and in spiritual openness.

2 | *The Meaning of Insight, Knowledge, and Wisdom in Buddhism*

In contrast to those religions that are based on unprovable articles of faith, the basis of Buddhism is *understanding*. This fact has misled some Western observers into considering Buddhism to be a purely rational doctrine that can be completely understood on purely intellectual principles. However, understanding in Buddhism means insight into the nature of reality, and is always the product of immediate experience.

Beginning with the experience of suffering as a primary, universally valid axiom, Buddhism adopts the standpoint that only what has been experienced, and not what has been thought out, has reality value. In this way the Buddha's Dharma proves itself to be a genuine religion, even though it does not appeal to unproven revelations derived from a supernatural realm such as the adherents of a faith-religion normally have to accept.

About the turn of this century Indologists tried to present Buddhism as a purely philosophical-moral system that was largely based on psychological considerations. But Buddhism is more than a philosophy, because it does not despise either reason or logic but merely uses them within their proper sphere. It also transcends the boundaries of any psychological system, because it is not confined to the analysis and classification of recognized psychic forces and phenomena, but also teaches their use, transformation, and transcending. Nor can Buddhism be reduced to a moral system valid for all time or a "guide to doing good," because it penetrates to a sphere beyond good and evil, to a sphere that transcends all dualism and is based on an ethic that grows out of the profoundest understanding and inner vision.

Thus we could say that the Buddha's Dharma is, as experience and as a way to practical realization, a *religion;* as the intellectual formulation of this experience, a *philosophy;* and as the result of systematic self-observation and analysis, a *psychology*. Whoever treads this path acquires a norm of behavior that is not dictated from without but is the result of an inner process of maturation and that we, regarding it from without, can call *morality*. But this morality in Buddhism is not—as in many other religions—the starting point so much as the outcome of a religious experience that has produced such a decisive change in our outlook that we begin to see the world with new eyes.

For this reason the Buddha placed at the beginning of the Noble Eightfold Path not any change in our way of life and behavior, but the dispassionate viewing of the world within and about us; for only so can we gain an unprejudiced insight into the nature of existence and of things, and then, through the change in our way of looking, achieve a complete reorientation of our striving. This way of seeing and observing things is called in Pali *sammā diṭṭhi* (Skt. *samyag-dṛṣṭi*), which the Indologists regularly translate as "right view" or "opinion."

But *sammā diṭṭhi* means more than a mere agreement with certain preconceived dogmatic or moral ideas. It is a way of seeing that goes beyond the dualistically conceived pairs of opposites of a one-sided, ego-conditioned standpoint. *Sammā* (Skt. *samyak*) means what is perfect or entire, that is, neither split nor one-sided; something, in fact, that is fully adequate to every level of consciousness.

Anyone who has developed *sammā diṭṭhi* is thus a person who does not look at things one-sidedly, but sees them dispassionately and without prejudice, and who in aims, deeds, and words is able to see and pay regard to the point of view of others as well as his own. For the Buddha was well aware of the relativity of all conceptual formulations. Accordingly, he was not concerned to proclaim an abstract truth but to present a method which should enable people themselves to break through to the vision of truth, that is, to the experiencing of reality. And so the Buddha proclaimed no new faith, but attempted rather to free people's thinking from the prejudices of dogmatic tenets, so as to make possible an unprejudiced viewing of reality.

It is clear that he was the first among mankind's great religious leaders and thinkers to make the discovery that what matters is not so much the formulated end results of human thought, that is, our conceptual knowledge in the form of ideas, religious confessions, and "eternal truths" or in the form of scientific "facts" and formulas, as that which leads to this knowledge, the *method* of thinking and acting. The adoption of the results of other people's thinking—or even of so-called "bare facts"—is, when this is done uncritically, generally a hindrance rather than an advantage, because it sets a block to direct experience, and can thus become a danger. And so an education that consists entirely of an accumulation of factual knowledge and ready-made thought patterns leads to spiritual sterility. Knowledge and faith that have lost their link with life turn into ignorance and superstition. The most important and essential thing is the capacity for concentration and creative thinking. Instead of aiming for erudition, we should preserve the capacity for *learning* itself, and so keep our minds open and receptive.

On the other hand, the Buddha never denied the importance of thinking and logic. But he assigned to thinking and logic the place that is fitting, and showed his disciples their relativity: the inextricable bond by which thinking and logic are contained in the system of mutual interdependence and conditionality.

There is a tacit assumption that the world we construct with our thought is identical with the world of our experience, in fact with the world "as such." But this is one of the principal sources of our erroneous view of what we call "world." The world that we experience indeed includes the world of our thought, but the world of our thought can never fully comprehend the world we experience, because we live simultaneously in various dimensions, of which that of the intellect (or the capacity for discursive thought) is only one.

When we intellectually reproduce experiences that by their nature belong to other dimensions, we are doing something similar to what the painter does when he represents three-dimensional space on a two-dimensional surface. He does this by deliberately forgoing certain qualities belonging to the higher dimension through the introduction of a new order of tonal values, proportions, and optical foreshortenings, which are only valid in the artistic unity of his picture and from a particular angle of vision. The laws of this perspective are essentially similar to the laws of logic: both sacrifice the qualities of a higher dimension by arbitrarily limiting themselves to a particular point of view, so that their objects are always seen only from one side and in a foreshortening and proportion appropriate to this angle of vision.

But whereas the painter consciously transfers his impressions from one dimension to another and has no intention of imitating or reproducing an objective reality, but rather wishes to express his *reaction* to that reality, the thinker generally falls into the trap of supposing he has grasped reality with his own thinking, because he mistakes the "foreshortening" perspective of his one-sided logic for universal law.

The use of logic for the process of thinking is undoubtedly just as necessary and justified as the use of perspective in painting, but only as a means of expression and not as a criterion of reality. In this sense the Buddha made use of thought in all his discourses, but he paid great attention to its boundaries, and accordingly also taught what went beyond thought: direct seeing (*sammā diṭṭhi*).

The Buddha did not seek blind followers who would carry out his instructions mechanically, without understanding their reason or necessity. For him the value of human action lay not in the outward effect, but in the *motive*, in the attitude of that consciousness from which it sprang. He wanted his disciples to follow him because of their own insight into the reality underlying his teaching, and not out of mere faith in the superiority of his wisdom or his person. The only faith he expected from his pupils was faith in their own inner powers. What he called forth in them, therefore, was not the emphasis on a cold, one-sided rationalism, but the harmonious cooperation of all the powers of the human psyche, among which reason is the discriminating and directing principle.

The Buddha's teaching begins with the presentation of the Four Noble Truths. But because of the narrow limits of the individual consciousness, their significance cannot be fully recognized when one enters on the path. If we were able to achieve this, liberation would be gained immediately and the remaining steps on the path would be unnecessary. But the simple fact of suffering and its immediate causes is something we can clearly experience in all phases of life, so that a simple process of observation and analysis of one's own experience, however limited, suffices to convince a thinking person of the reasonableness and acceptability of the Buddha's thesis. Accordingly, if he makes his path begin with the demand for "perfect view," this does not mean the acceptance of a particular dogma established for all time, or of some tenet or article of faith, but the unprejudiced and impartial insight into the nature of things and of all occurrences, *just as they are*.

Sammā diṭṭhi, then, is no mere believing acceptance of some preconceived religious or moral ideas. *Sammā diṭṭhi* means rather an increasingly perfected, not one-sided way of viewing things. For is it not true that so much trouble in the world arises principally from the fact that everyone sees things from his own vantage point? Should we not, instead of closing our senses against everything unpleasant and painful, look the fact of suffering in the face and so find its cause, which lies in ourselves, and which consequently can only be overcome by ourselves?

If we proceed in this way, there dawns within us the awareness of the lofty goal, the goal of enlightenment and liberation, and also of the path that leads to its realization. *Sammā diṭṭhi* is thus the *experiencing*, and not just the intellectual acceptance, of the Four Noble Truths proclaimed by the Buddha. It is only from such an attitude that the perfect resolve that embraces the whole human being (Pali *sammā sankappa*) can be born, which demands the commitment of the whole person in thought, word, and deed, and which leads through complete internalization and penetration to perfect enlightenment.

As we have already remarked, the full significance of the Four Noble Truths cannot be immediately perceived when one first enters upon the path. In this sense the Buddha's teaching is also to some extent metaphysical and, as such, requires some confidence on the part of the person who feels drawn to it, confidence (Skt. *śraddhā*, Pali *saddhā*) in the rightness of what one who has only just started on the path cannot yet know by experience. In other words, Buddhism too must at first demand from its followers the trusting acceptance of certain teachings that lie beyond the range of experience of a beginner, just as every science and, still more, every religion must do.

However, there is a difference between revealed religions and science on the one hand, and Buddhism on the other, a difference rooted in psychology. The first two lay stress on a sphere that lies outside of the individual's experience, because they depend on the authority of tradition, or of experimentation, and the tacit assumptions associated with these. Buddhism, on the other hand, places the stress on the interior of the individual, in which personal experience must prove the truth of what is at first taken on trust. Here there is no justification by faith (in the sense of acceptance of an unproven dogma), but a becoming conscious of that reality that remains metaphysical for us only so long as we have not experienced it for ourselves.

Buddhism, then, is when seen from without a system of metaphysics (among other things), but when seen from within—as an expression of what has been experienced—it is empirical. The Buddha never rejected anything metaphysical that can be discovered on the path of inner experience, but on the other hand he had no use for philosophico-metaphysical speculation. However, he overcame speculative metaphysics and its problems not by mere rejection, but positively, by extending the boundaries of the experienceable: by training, expanding, and intensifying consciousness, by which means the metaphysical became empirical.

The training of consciousness is therefore an inescapable prerequisite to higher understanding. Consciousness is the vessel on which the receptivity of the individual depends, and it is through previous perceptions that the selection of material to be accepted and the direction of its penetration are determined. Wakefulness, attentiveness, and mindfulness (Skt. *smṛti,* Pali *sati*) are absolutely necessary in order not to fall into the trap of suggestion from within or without.

Apart from this, the existence of a tradition is necessary in which the experiences and perceptions of previous generations are formulated, because otherwise each individual would be compelled to gain afresh all possible psychic and spiritual discoveries and experiences, as a result of which only very few specially gifted individuals would succeed in reaching the goal of enlightenment. But the knowledge or intellectual assimilation of the results achieved by previous seekers after truth, and set forth in terms of philosophy, is insufficient. Thus even the perfect formulation of the doctrine by the Buddha did not relieve his successors of the necessity of reformulation. For although he had formulated his teaching perfectly, the people to whom he proclaimed this teaching were not perfect, with the result that what they understood and passed on corresponded to their own mental level.

We must also remember that the Buddha was compelled to make use of the language and popular notions of his time, in order to be understood. And even if all those who heard the word of the Buddha and preserved it were really perfectly enlightened, as tradition has it, that would still not alter the fact that the intellectual and linguistic form in which they passed on the teaching was conditioned by their time. Therefore, they could not anticipate problems that had not yet arisen. And even if they had been able to anticipate such problems, the language in which they would have had to express both the problems and the answers had not been developed, and would not have been understood even if they had spontaneously invented it.

The Buddha would undoubtedly have expressed his teaching differently if, instead of living in the sixth century B.C.E., he had lived in the twentieth century, but not because the truth to be proclaimed (the Dharma) was any different. Rather, the people to whom he would have preached his doctrine have added twenty-five centuries of historical, practical, and spiritual experience to their consciousness. This consciousness therefore commands not only a greater store of concepts and ways of expression, it also has a quite different attitude of mind, with different perspectives and problems, and with new possibilities of solution appropriate to this mentality.

Those who believe blindly in words, and equally those for whom historical antiquity or the sanctity of tradition is more important than truth are naturally unwilling to accept this fact, which robs their nicely delimited worldview, ready-made for home use, of its absolute validity and unambiguous certainty. They therefore imagine that the later Buddhist schools have altered the Buddha's teaching by wilfully overstepping its boundaries.

In fact, however, these successors of the Buddha simply left behind the limited and temporally conditioned conceptions of the Buddha's contemporary pupils, who had sought to fix his teaching once for all. But thought can no more be fixed than life itself. And where growth ceases, only the dead form remains. What we are left with is a mummified historical curiosity, but not the life that once filled it. Those who stress the authenticity of the form should ask themselves whether it is possible to carry the forms of past millennia into the present just as they were. Even food, if kept for too long, turns to poison. And the same thing applies to mental food—truth turns to dogma and faith to superstition. Both of these things are dead, and so they become hindrances to thought and experiencing, and thus a deadly poison.

Truths cannot be taken on trust. They need to be continually rediscovered and formed afresh if they are to retain their spiritual content, their life and nutritive value. It is a law of spiritual growth that the same truths must be continually experienced and thought through in new forms. It is not so much a matter of the results that previous ages have gained, as of the underlying methods by which we ever and anew come to an understanding, and *that* is what we have to cultivate and pass on.

In living afresh through this process of growth, each individual becomes a link between past and present, completes the past through present experience, and prepares the creative seeds of the future. It is only through such an attitude that the past acquires a value for the present and becomes a part of our own knowledge instead of a mere object of study which, being divorced from the organic process of growth, loses its reality content.

When once we have grasped this organic process of growth and becoming, we stop calling its separate phases "right" or "wrong," "valuable" or "worthless." In fact we find that the variations on the same theme, through the strength of the contrast in emphasis and modulation, bring out the common or essential underlying factor, and thus lead us to an understanding that encourages us, not to narrowness and intolerance, but to a viewpoint that stands above the differences, and thus to spiritual openness and tolerance.

This does not exclude the possibility that as individuals we feel more strongly drawn to one or the other current within the Buddhist sphere of development, and that particular features of one school appeal to us more than those of another, in accordance with our temperament, our gifts, our understanding, and our present stage of development. But such a preference should never lead us into condemning what does not fit into our own personal scheme, and still less do we have the right to declare that the tradition of our chosen school is the only genuine and true one.

It should therefore be the task of Buddhism in the West to create an understanding of the whole development of Buddhism, thus enabling an overall view of the organic growth of those fundamental ideas that the Buddha once planted as seeds in the hearts of his disciples. Under the conditions of the most varied cultures and climatic conditions, and in conformity with the mentality of different races and cultures, these developed in multifarious forms, but without abandoning the essential content of buddhahood and not, in the process, losing its characteristic "flavor"—that of liberation, enlightenment, and universality.

Already on Indian soil there arose in the first thousand years of Buddhism three great Buddhist schools, each of which laid special stress on one of the three above-mentioned aspects. Thus under the aspect of "liberation from suffering" that school arose that rejected the world on account of its inconstancy. This standpoint led to a certain retreat from the world. People tried to evade suffering by avoiding all contact with normal life. It is on this conception that the institution of monasticism is founded.

A second school stressed the second aspect of the Dharma: enlightenment as the sole worthy goal for a follower of the Exalted One, even if this meant that we should have to take upon ourselves the suffering of the whole world because we identified with the suffering of all beings. In this way the entire world was drawn into the process of liberation, and suffering was overcome by compassion, a compassion so all-embracing that all personal sorrow becomes meaningless unless as a spur on the way to the supreme goal.

This great compassion (Skt. *mahākaruṇa*) is the direct expression of the spirit of enlightenment (*bodhicitta*) developing within a person. It is not based on any fleeting wave of emotion, but is a turning toward all beings that ripens through love (*maitrī*) and wisdom (*prajñā*)—their suffering being felt as one's own. Love makes possible a spontaneous "making oneself equal to the other" without allowing any feelings of moral or spiritual superiority to arise. And wisdom enables us to perceive the conditioned origination of all phenomena in mutual dependence, and lets us experience the "egolessness" (*anātman*) of all elements of reality; it leads us to an understanding of emptiness, to the realization of the way all beings are bound up with one another, and so opens up for us the path of bodhisattvahood, which can be undertaken independently of any particular way of life, by householders and monks alike.

The third aspect of Buddhism, that of universality, stresses the psychological consequences that arise from the potential and fundamental universality of the individual consciousness. Further, it points out the possibility of converting every feature of the human personality into a means of achieving liberation, including those that at first appear to be obstacles on the path. In this way every expression of life becomes an expression of the fundamental unity of *saṃsāra* and *nirvāṇa* and makes clear the interrelation of physical and mental characteristics, of the sensual and the transcendental, the individual and the universal.

These three aspects of Buddhism, which in the course of its historical development made their appearance with varying degrees of emphasis, correspond to the three traditional "vehicles" (*yānas*) which lead to liberation, and which are known in the history of

Buddhism as the "small," the "great," and the "diamond vehicle" (*Hīnayāna, Mahāyāna, Vajrayāna*).

The step from the small to the great vehicle took place through that change in inner attitude whereby the desire for individual liberation from a world of transience was replaced (on the basis of the recognition of the essential equality of all beings at the highest level of consciousness) by the conception of a transformable world. The step from the "great vehicle" to the "diamond vehicle" was the consequence of the recognition of the transformability of the world, and of the knowledge of the relativity of *saṃsāra* and *nirvāṇa* as two aspects of one and the same reality. This led to the refinement and differentiation of the practical methods of transformation, which included all psychic factors in man—in particular, the limitless possibilities of his consciousness—through which the individual becomes aware of his universality and so brings about the realization of his overriding wholeness.

Hīnayāna, Mahāyāna, and Vajrayāna thus represent three dimensions of mind, in which each successive one does not abolish the previous one but includes its qualities and integrates them on a higher plane or in a network of further-reaching relations. In this way the ethical principles (Pali *sīla*, Skt. *śīla*) of the small vehicle, together with the basic truths of Buddhism (Pali *cattāri ariya-saccāni*, Skt. *catvāri ārya-satyāni*) are the foundation on which the Mahāyana erected its high philosophy (*Prajñāpāramitāvāda, Śūnyavāda, Vijñānavāda,*, etc.). And again, the Vajrayāna integrated the Mahāyāna philosophy (*prajñā*) and the Hīnayāna discipline and ethics (*śīla*) and made them the basis of its specific systems of meditation and yoga-practice in order thus to achieve the inner transformation and unification (*samādhi*).

Śīla, prajñā, and *samādhi*—the three principles of the Noble Eightfold Path of liberation—can thus be regarded as the characteristics of the three vehicles, Hīnayāna, Mahāyāna, and Vajrayāna. Each one of these three vehicles includes all three principles, but each is distinguished from the others by giving precedence to one or other of these principles, and by giving to this principle that is emphasized a particular significance and a new interpretation in accordance with the attitude of the school concerned. Thus, to generalize, we could say that the attitude of the small vehicle is realistic and analytic, that of the great vehicle idealistic and monistic, while the diamond vehicle developed an integral system of psycho-cosmic relations, developing on this basis meditative practices that produce a profound transformation of the human personality by working on the deep layers of the psyche.

The Hīnayāna teaches us to see the world as it is (*yathābhūtaṃ*), without enquiring about the objective reality and substantiality of the world. On the other hand, it teaches that the world, in the form in which we experience it, is enclosed "in this fathom-long body." But both body and world are experienced as painful. In the Mahāyāna the world is stripped of its character of reality in favor of an abstract, transcendental datum, without qualities or names, which can only be indicated by the term *śūnyatā*, an "emptiness" not rationally graspable, which at the same time denotes endless potentiality. In the Vajrayāna, the analytical realism of the Hīnayāna and the abstract-metaphysical idealism of the Mahāyāna philosophy are balanced through creative imagery and inner vision, by means of which the entire human personality is transformed by a process of continuous integration.

The Vajrayāna represents the final phase of development of Buddhism in its native India. It represents in a sense the integration of all previous developments in Buddhism. Thus here *śūnyatā*—the great "emptiness" free from all qualifications—is recognized as the primal quality of consciousness, which is itself the final instance of all knowledge and creative realization. It is not possible, either through thought or by experience, to go beyond consciousness, so that even that which we denote with the label "enlightenment" is a phenomenon of consciousness. From this it is clear that "reality" is neither an abstract "suchness" nor a fixed, absolute principle, but is rather the working of consciousness as a living force that brings forth and embraces all things. It is only to the extent that the individual consciousness becomes aware of its potential and primeval universality, that there comes an expansion of its experience of reality, of the intensity of its perceptions, and the cosmogonic power of creative world-formation, world transformation, integrative fusion, and wholeness.

Whereas the early Hīnayāna schools regarded the body as an unavoidable evil—like a wound that one has to treat with care in order to get rid of it as quickly as possible—the Vajrayāna shows us the body as a microcosm, as an image of the universe, and as the vessel of transformation, in which all the higher powers lie waiting to be awakened. It is the great *maṇḍala*, the "magic circle" in which the great transformation takes place.

Thus the Hīnayāna teaches us to observe the continual change and alteration in the phenomenal world. The Mahāyāna leads us on to the recognition of the transformability of that world, while the Vajrayāna teaches us the practice of transformation within and out of the fullness of life. Thus the way through the great schools of Buddhism leads from suffering because of impermanence, through compassion for all beings, to the acceptance of suffering as a means of purification and liberation from the bonds of egocentricity. In order to experience the whole of Buddhism in and for himself, each person who wishes to tread the Buddhist path should develop the phases of this process with understanding and through experience. For this purpose the sympathetic guidance of an understanding friend is necessary, taking in both the intellectual and the emotional powers of a person.

We have already pointed to the danger of being caught up in pure historicity, orthodoxy, and intellectualism. It is only through the development of perfect view (*samyag-dṛṣṭi*) that we can avoid this peril; but it is not a matter of "right" or "wrong" opinions or views in the intellectual sense, but of direct, intuitive insight into the true nature of things and especially into the nature of what we call our "I." However, if such an intuition does not produce a corresponding change in our thinking, it will never have any real influence on our lives, because no power can become effective unless it is shaped and directed to a goal.

On the other hand, thoughts and observations that have been one-sidedly developed on the intellectual plane must be confirmed by direct experience if they are to have the power and ability to change our lives and our inmost being. Whoever dwells exclusively in the realm of thought remains a prisoner of his thought, just as one who clings to more or less vague intuitions or waves of feeling is a prisoner of his momentary moods and emotions. It is therefore necessary to harmonize and coordinate one's thoughts and emotions. Only the person who succeeds in doing this enjoys the liberty of the intuitive spirit, and can work unhindered by preconceived opinions and prejudices. Such a person alone is able, rejoicing in creative joy and satisfaction, to build up an all-embracing worldview out of the elements of intuitive experience, to develop and expand it continually until he attains the breakthrough to perfect enlightenment.

Thus there is no necessity to deny our intellect, or to repress the free flow of our thoughts and the capacity for intelligent consideration (*vitarka-vicāra*), as long as we are conscious of the boundaries of our discursive thought and apply our intellect within the boundaries of its appropriate sphere. Within this sphere the capacity for consistent thought is a valuable tool of the human mind. Without its directing, clarifying, and stabilizing qualities, our life would turn into a chaotic nightmare. But if it makes itself independent, it creates a world of illusion that closes all the doors of experience and blocks all paths of spiritual unfoldment.

When we start the study of the Buddhist Dharma, we should remember that this teaching is based on actual knowledge and experience. Its sole purpose is to stimulate all who come into contact with it to experience for themselves. For while the thinker may succeed in understanding the world indirectly, through the mediation of intellectual systems with the aid of concepts and logical deductions, real experience provides a direct approach to the intuitive holistic awareness which the one who has experienced it can then describe with the aid of logic.

Western logic operates largely with abstract concepts without being aware that the logic of language is only one among many possibilities of logical and consistent thinking. People operate with words and concepts as if these were the direct expression of reality. It was from just such a false position that Kant was able to postulate the "thing in itself" ("*Ding an sich*"), which like every absolute exists only in thought, as an abstraction from that reality that presents itself to our senses.

The "thing in itself," then, is a limit-value of logical-analytical thought, something that in reality (i.e., outside of the thinker) does not exist. For there is no "thing" that "in itself" exists. Every thing arises and consists only in dependent relation to other things, embedded in continually changing relations. And it is only in this sense that we speak in Buddhism of "relativity," not equating the concept "relative" with "only apparent"; rather it points to the essential nature of all phenomenal forms, which arise, operate, and cease in conditional dependence and mutual relationship.

Thus, for instance, the relativity of time is by no means a proof of its unreality, but rather proof of its manifold variety. Thus the same thing, considered from various points of view, appears different. And therefore no "thing in itself" exists, it exists only in the context of and in dependence on other things, that is, in a continually changing field of ever varying relations to the most disparate phenomenal forms.

From the Buddhist point of view the conception of a "pure reason" must be rejected, because it stands in a certain contradiction to experienced reality, and the same applies to abstract logic to which absolute validity is ascribed. In the course of history various systems of logic have been developed, for instance a Western, Indian, Chinese, and Japanese logic. Each of these forms of logic is consistent in its way, and whichever one we choose as our starting point, as long as our system remains consistent, we can call our procedure logical.

Western logic is based on duality, that is, it is binary and two-dimensional, as is expressed in the "law of contradiction." Indian logic is based on a fourfold proposition: "It is," "it is not," "it is not, and yet it is," "it is, and yet it is not." Chinese logic, again, is not bound to words but to images or symbols that stand as ciphers for complexes of meaning. On the other hand, Japanese logic arises from a strong attachment to nature, and employs corresponding analogies.

However, within the same cultural spheres there have always been some people with a different way of thinking and understanding the world. While the thinkers of the West lived for the most part in a world of abstract concepts, or moved in a world of "pure ideas," the really great scientists and artists were concerned to understand the processes of life holistically by observation and thought. But understanding implies identifying with the other, putting oneself in the other's place, or, in other words, being capable of transformation.

The world appears to us as a field of polarities that at first appear to us as oppositions, such as light and darkness, near and far, cold and warm, noise and quiet, good and evil, which we cannot simply explain away. Nor should we try to expel the one in favor of the other, or attempt to convert the world as a whole to one or the other extreme. It is important, rather, to find the creative center in this field of force, in order thus to bring about the cooperative action of the opposites, which results from their already existing mutually conditioning relation and interdependence.

Let us make this clear with an example. A violin string connects two opposed fixed points. If it is stretched too tightly, it produces a shrill note like a shriek. But if it is not taut enough, we get no sound at all. If, however, the correct tension is achieved between the fixed points, so that the string is neither too taut nor too loose, then we obtain a clear and harmonious note. In just the same way, in the mental sphere it is necessary to find the correct tensional relation while avoiding the extremes of slackness and excessive tenseness.

The dynamism of the universe depends largely on the interplay of the forces of attachment and freedom. Attachment appears in the form of resistance to change, and can be defined both as "constancy" and as "inertia factor." In addition, attachment operates also as a centripetal force in the form of attraction, both in the microcosm and in the macrocosm. Freedom, on the other hand, appears as a tendency to move forward, to changing positions or conditions, which we experience as inconstancy, continual change, or alteration, and we recognize it in the microcosm and the macrocosm as centrifugal force. The outcome of attachment and freedom in the universe is a movement that combines transformability with constancy, that is to say, a circular or spiral movement that returns to its starting point—a movement, in short, that is predictable and not arbitrary. It displays constancy in change, and thus denotes not destruction but transformation, that is, change in accordance with indwelling law.

Thus, all the heavenly bodies turn on their own axis and follow an elliptical path. They never move in a straight line. Motions in a straight line are purely constructions of abstract thinking. Only abstract thinking could invent the "unchanging," the "eternal," and elevate it into an ideal. And yet it is in just this abstract thinking that practically all religions originate. They are based on wishful thinking, deceive humanity with false promises that are contrary to nature and observable fact. But the worst thing is that they make man believe he alone is an exception to the laws of nature and is in possession of an "immortal" soul that outlasts all changes and transformations and is possessed by no other living beings.

Indian thought, on the other hand, regarded every being and thing as a unique expression of the whole, to which it is linked by a multiplicity of relations. This is the kind of "relativity" of which the Buddha spoke. Whatever is postulated outside of these relations, whatever is unrelated, is unreal, because it exists only as something conceived and has no relation to reality. It is therefore contrary to all reason to speak of an "absolute," which is a pure abstract speculation and is only employed by those who wish to avoid giving a definition because they are unable to make any genuine statement.

Nāgārjuna was therefore only being consistent when he applied the fundamental perception of the Buddha, that all Dharmas (all the elements of reality) are "non-self" (*anātman*), to everything objective. But this was not a "re-Hinduization" of Buddhism (as some modern Indian writers of the school of Radhakrishnan have declared), but simply an argument against the Sarvāstivādin idea that assigned the "nature of being" to the Dharmas (*sarva asti* "everything is"), which seemed to contradict the teaching of the Buddha that "all elements of existence are not-self" (Pali *sabbe dhammā anattā*). I say "seemed," because everything that we perceive exists purely as perception, since no substantiality adheres to it. It exists, thus understood, as a continually self-repeating phenomenon. But if we start from a concept of substance, then we have to agree logically that nothing exists "in an absolute sense" (i.e., outside of our sphere of perception), and that, therefore, everything is in its nature *śūnya*, that is, empty of any monadic self-nature in the sense of the Hindu *ātman* doctrine.

The fact that Hinduism subsequently adopted a modified form of *śūnyavāda*, making Nāgārjuna's philosophy the basis of its Advaita system by turning *śūnyatā* into an absolute, is not the fault of Nāgārjuna but of Śaṅkarācārya, who twisted Nāgārjuna's teaching into his Advaita philosophy, which he then applied to the Vedas without admitting that he had wrongfully plagiarized Nāgārjuna's *śūnyavāda*. In order to cover this up, he slandered Buddhism and made crude attacks on the Buddha, thus putting himself outside the tolerance traditionally observed in the Indian region. Śaṅkarācārya was certainly a great scholar, but he was an even greater plagiarist. Anyone who makes Nāgārjuna out to be a quasi "re-Hinduizing falsifier of Buddhism," and interprets Nāgārjuna's *śūnyatā** as an absolute, has not understood the difference between the Buddhist Advaya doctrine and the Hindu Advaita.

By the expression *śūnyatā*, Nāgārjuna wanted to demonstrate the nonapplicability of all concepts and the impossibility of grasping philosophically the highest reality, since this consists only in the experience of the whole and the unlimited relationships per-

---

*Nāgārjuna always regards the conception of *śūnyatā* as "emptiness of . . . ," and the *concept* of *śūnyatā* must be seen as empty *(śūnyatā-śūnyatā)*.

ceived in this; therefore, *śūnyatā* is free from all conceptual definition, and it embraces omnirelativity.

The key to the understanding of Nāgārjuna's *mādhyamaka-śūnyavāda* doctrine, that is, his doctrine of the middle way and of the emptiness of all definitions, lies in *pratītya-samutpāda*, the well-known formula of conditioned and simultaneous arising, of the act with continuing results, and of the interlinking and interconnection of all things and conditions. This basic attitude excludes any belief in an absolute, as well as all speculation, since this always moves outside the realm of experience, and it makes clear that Buddhism is a system shaped by experience, which concerns itself only with the actual in the sense of that which is *active*, and not with the results of speculative thought. This self-imposed rejection of speculation gives Buddhism a universal validity and a freedom from theological dogmatism, which is based on mere belief and wishful thinking.

Buddhism has never denied the possibility of higher levels of consciousness or higher spiritual forms of life. But it concerns itself solely with what is attainable for us, not with purely speculative theories about gods, or about an almighty creator of the universe who is only an imaginary ideal of our own personality inflated to infinity. On the other hand, the Buddha never raised any objection to the belief in a god or gods if this made the believer a better person. And he never argued about theological problems. He was atheistic neither in the sense of nihilism nor in that of materialism, and he was not a monotheist. Nor did he profess any kind of idealistic or materialistic monism, but rather allowed everybody to keep their own convictions, because he knew that it is not important what people *believe*—the decisive thing is what they *do*. But what they do must conform to what they believe, in other words, to what they preach and how they live.

But what does Buddhism mean by action? The Buddha himself gave the definition. According to this, action is not the same as an external deed, but is always what we do intentionally and in full awareness. What distinguishes action (in this sense) from the external deed is the will that underlies it. Only such a conscious doing is the effective act, karma, born of *cetanā*, the voluntary decision that is the motive of the action. It is only in this way that we can understand what Nāgasena, in *Milinda's Questions*, means when he says that a man who kills without intent is no murderer, but that someone who thrusts a sword through a beehive in the belief that it is a human being is, because of this intention, karmically guilty of murder. Thus it is intention that makes an action karmically neutral, wholesome, or unwholesome.

The Buddha's worldview is based on the recognition that all existence is subject to continual change and that this change takes place according to a law that is of universal application. This rule of law is made visible in *pratītya-samutpāda,* in the doctrines of karma and rebirth, in the moral responsibility of human beings, and in the freedom of individual decision that this implies.

The Pali concept of *anicca* (Skt. *anitya*), which we here translate as "change," is generally equated with "transience." Its real meaning is "not lasting" or "not eternal." It therefore incorporates not only the negative concept of transience, but also the forward-pointing, creative concept of becoming, of becoming something new and different. If therefore we suffer pain as a result of our attempt to stay put, hold on, and cling to what eludes us, this is not the fault of the world but a result of our own wrong attitude, conditioned by selfishness, to existing conditions. The Buddha's aim was to make clear to us this already existing reality, so that we might recognize and accept it. He therefore rejects all belief that is merely based on wishful fantasies and does not correspond to the truth of unprejudiced experience.

Reality is, as we have seen, a process of continual change and transformation. Nothing can escape this process, not even what we call our "ego," our "soul," or our "self." It is therefore absurd to speak of transmigration of souls (*Seelenwanderung*) in Buddhism. If we really must use some such term, then at most we may use the term "transformation of souls" (*Seelenwandlung*). But "soul" in this context means not an immortal, eternal, changeless monad, but the sum, or better, the totality of the psychic impulses, just as Buddhism has taught them for thousands of years and as they are now also recognized by modern psychology.

What raised the Buddha's Dharma high above the multifarious spiritual life of his time was the recognition of the dynamic nature of reality that he had gained through the enlightenment experience. Looking back, he now saw the world (from the ordinary person's point of view) in a reversed perspective, from the standpoint of "nonself," seen from which the world dissolves into a stream of arising and vanishing elements of existence *(dharmas),* to which concepts such as "being" and "not-being" no longer apply. When the Buddha placed the *anātman* idea at the center of his teaching, he moved from a static conception of the world (as in the Upaniṣads) to a dynamic one; from placing a stress on being (Skt. *sat*) to placing it on becoming (Skt. *bhāva*), from the conception of a permanent "self" to the recognition of the mutual relationship of all that exists within the process of the conditioned genesis of all the phenomena of life—from a purely mechanical process of development to the ability of the individual to grow beyond itself.

And so here, from the Upaniṣadic belief in a transmigration of souls we come to the experiential certainty of a transformation of souls. But it is just here that many Western Buddhists are in difficulties. They want to speak of "rebirth without a soul." But that is just as illogical as it would be to speak of "psychology without a psyche." Let us finally make an end of the prejudice of the early European Buddhists, who equated the "soul" with the idea of a separate, unchanging ego or self, thereby robbing us of a word as beautiful as it is profound, and which, like the Greek *psyche*, denotes the totality and organic wholeness of all the spiritual powers that work and grow within us.

It is often stated that the majority of Western Buddhists regard the idea of rebirth simply as a working hypothesis. Those who say this do not realize that most of those who have come to Buddhism did so because they were convinced of the fact of rebirth and of its underlying rule of law (karma). For without this conviction, the Buddhist teaching becomes senseless, because death would then automatically mean total obliteration and extinction, which would render all striving pointless.

In Buddhism, the term *anātman* occupies a central position. *Anātman* in Buddhism means the nonabsoluteness, the nonselfhood of all elements of reality and all phenomena, and thus their boundlessness, their all-relatedness, and their potential for transformation. This capacity for change and fluidity alone is life; immobility and rigidity mean death. The more we want to persist in our "own being," the more certainly we deliver ourselves up to death. For that which we call "being" is a continual, conditioned becoming and ceasing, a process of transformation in which there is neither a remaining the same nor a difference, neither a coming to be in the sense of a first beginning, nor a vanishing in the sense of absolute destruction.

Buddhism reveals relativity in the sense of endless relations and possibilities of a relation, not relativity in the sense of relativization and thus diminution of an existing value or phenomenon. The formula of dependent and simultaneous origination, which can be interpreted both temporally and spatially, that is, both causally and beyond all relations of time and place, and thus synchronistically, was in the past often presented both by scholars who did not penetrate its profundity, and by interpreters of all shades who remained at a superficial level, as a "causal formula." In this way they thought to give Buddhism a "scientific" stamp. It did not occur to them that causality and synchronicity are not necessarily mutually exclusive—a point to which the Buddha himself returned when he declared that *pratītya-samutpāda* was to be understood in a much deeper sense and not merely as a simple chain of causality in space and time, namely as the internal dependence of every phenomenal form on every other. When Ānanda (*Dīgha Nikāya* 15) declared that the formula of dependent origination was easy to understand and intellectually satisfying, thus interpreting it in a purely temporal-causal sense, the Buddha rebuked him and referred to its profound and difficult-to-comprehend sense.

This *pratītya-samutpāda* was at all times regarded as one of the central doctrines of Buddhism. Nāgārjuna made it, as we can see from his introductory *kārikās,* the basis of his Mādhyamaka philosophy. In so doing, he freed the formula of dependent origination from a one-sided, time-and-space–oriented interpretation, and thus restored the deeper meaning of the word *sam-utpāda** in the sense originally intended by the Buddha. Thus understood, the formula can be taken both causally and also in a synchronistic-conditional sense. This also explains why the Buddha did not always keep to the strict sequence of the chain from the first to the last member of the twelvefold form of *pratītya-samutpāda,* thereby making clear the relativity of the temporal sequence. And thus Nāgārjuna could rightly say:

> Without arising and without disappearing,
> Not eternal, not cut off,
> Neither identical nor different,
> Without going or coming.
> He who teaches thus dependent and simultaneous arising,
> The quiet quenching of all arguments,

**Śamutpāda* (Pali *samuppāda*) = "arising, origin": *sam-*, prefix denoting wholeness and union; *utpāda* = "arising, appearing."

> Before the Enlightened One, best of all teachers,
> I prostrate myself.†

Once we have recognized and accepted these premises, we then have a good and safe starting point for our studies. We shall be able to grasp the essential nature of the Buddha-Dharma, and we can safely enter on our meditative path. Buddhism has always regarded thinking as our sixth sense and taught us its proper use. But people's thinking today has largely broken away. Our thinking has become "thinking about thinking," thinking at second hand, if not third or fourth hand. It has lost its immediacy and thereby its capacity to work with the symbols directly presented by life.

So now we have to return to make full use of the possibilities of our thought by applying it correctly, for the intellect that stops halfway is the greatest obstacle to spiritual progress. It is only when we have succeeded in transcending the bounds of thought with thought, when the intellect regards itself self-critically, that it becomes a valuable aid in the spiritual life. Then it is like the rudder of a ship, which can only work when the ship is in motion and is powerless when the motive power is lacking. Thus, intellect and thought are only of value when a psychic impulse derived from inner experience impels them, that is, as long as the individual is making spiritual progress and seeking to advance beyond his present spiritual state. It is only when there is such a motion as this that thinking can fulfill its legitimate functions, which are to order, to distinguish, to make a critical choice, and to maintain the chosen direction.

A person driven only by the emotions is like a rudderless ship. And one who is caught up in thinking alone is like a ship without power, whose rudder finds nothing to get a grip on and exhausts itself in an aimless back-and-forth motion like a disengaged cogwheel. And the person whose thinking stops halfway is—to continue the image—like a helmsman who turns the steering wheel only to one side, so that his ship keeps going around in circles. But this is just the way that the average man uses his capacity for thought. If we want to overcome this condition, we must not throw

---

† Anirodham anutpādam
Anucchedam aśaśvataṃ
Anekārtam anānārtham
Anāgamam anirgamaṃ
Yah pratītyasamutpādaṃ
Prapañcopaśamaṃ śivaṃ
Deśayāmāsa sambuddhas
Taṃ vande vadatāṃ varaṃ.

our intellect overboard, but must make a more complete, that is, less one-sided, use of it by freeing our thought from its customary channels and learning to make full use of it to the limit of its possibilities. Only in this way can we break through the monotony of the deadly circle and relate to all that exists, in order finally to find the courage, having reached the limit of what we can think and imagine, to risk the leap into the wholeness of our own being.

If we wish to overcome our limited intellectual attitude, we must first of all develop our power of thought and our capacity for discrimination to the full; it is not possible to transcend an intellect one has never had or never controlled. Thought is just as necessary for the overcoming of mere emotionalism and mental confusion as intuition is needful for transcending intellectual limitations and conceptual attachments.

It seems paradoxical that Zen, the Far Eastern Buddhist meditation school that stresses the irrational most strongly, appeals more to intellectuals than to nonintellectuals. However, Zen like all schools of Buddhism, does have a rational basis. It depends neither on faith nor on petrified dogmas, but solely on direct experience and unprejudiced observation. Nevertheless, as a *Buddhist* school, Zen is based on the insights common to *all* Buddhist schools, without which Zen would not be "Zen." This common basis rests on experience, that is, on that area where science and mysticism meet. The only difference between those two fields of experience is that the truth of science—being directed toward external objects—is "objectively" provable or, better, demonstrable, whereas mysticism, being directed toward the subject, rests on "subjective" experience.

Like all Buddhist schools, Zen holds aloof from preconceived opinions, dogmas, and articles of faith, together with everything that generally goes by the name of "religion." This attitude was what impressed those people of our time who tend toward a scientific, antireligious attitude. The extreme individualism of the Zen method, which stands out more strongly than in any other Buddhist school, impressed the intellectuals as much as the fact that Zen cultivates beauty and a feeling for nature, a fact that appeals to the modern aesthete. But just because Zen meets the modern taste halfway, there is a danger of superficial judgment, of borrowing merely the external forms of expression, which fails to do justice to the inner content.

Quite early in the history of Buddhism, the attempt was made to break through the bounds of thought by means of paradox. The entire Mahāyāna literature is full of such things, for instance the *Prajñāpāramitā Sūtras*, the stories of the *siddhas*, and many formulations in the Tantric texts. But all these paradoxes were merely for the purpose of shaking up our thinking and freeing it from its accustomed patterns of conventional ideas and petrified dogmas. That alone is their meaning, their use, and their spiritual value. But if thinking in paradoxes becomes a kind of intellectual game, it fails in its purpose and leads only to cynicism and the destruction of all values.

This is where the old Buddhist schools part company from the modern intellectual attitude, which boasts of its freedom from religious and traditional values. All Buddhist schools, including Ch'an and Zen, have always stressed the dignity and value of all human beings and of all living beings, however insignificant some of these may appear, because they saw in every form of life an exponent of the all, in its way a unique expression, a point of intersection of all the lines of force. This was the way of Buddhism in all its schools—neither agnostic nor libertine, as modern man, having lost faith in himself and the world, so often is. Therefore a Buddhism for the present day and pointing to the future must again and again bring these ancient and profound convictions before the consciousness of mankind—convictions born of the experience of the cosmic order (*dharma*) and of the significance that pervades it (which should not be confused with the "purpose" of a teleological system), in which the experience of the individual is just as important as the abstract law.

It is high time the West realized that the unconventional aspect of various Mahāyāna schools can only be understood against the background of a profound metaphysical tradition that was so much alive that it could afford to discard conventional concepts. The rejection of religious dogmas and traditional forms (by, for instance, the *siddhas*) was the outcome neither of skepticism nor of a delight in shocking other people by outrageous words and actions, but stemmed from an inner certainty born of a profound experience of reality. People only "believe" in certain things when they are not sure about them. Nobody needs to "believe" in the sun, because everybody sees it, feels its warmth, and lives in its light. In the same way, a Buddhist will not doubt the values of religious experience, though possibly he may be dubious about many methods that have been used in history.

Thus it is the task of the Buddhist schools of our time to open up for people of the present age a direct approach to those values and powers that form the fundamental basis of all culture, religion, and meditative practice. But if people who have lost all connection with these powers and values try to apply methods like Ch'an, Zen, and Vajrayāna in a spiritual vacuum, they will hardly be able to advance beyond a species of intellectual hobby or playacting combined with a shallow aestheticism. In that case Ch'an, Zen, or the teaching of the *siddhas* will just be an excuse for living the way one has always lived, merely using a new label for the same behavior as before. In this way lack of self-control is dignified as spontaneity, weakness becomes nonviolence, laziness is made into the ideal of nonaction, and lack of logic is claimed to be spiritual profundity and declared to be "transcending conceptual thought," while emotionalism and wild fantasy are supposed to be "inspiration."

If therefore—in the framework of a presentation of the entire Buddhist tradition—we include Ch'an, Zen, and the teachings of the *siddhas* as being essential within our spiritual discipline and methodology, this can only be successful if our proceedings are based on a genuine religious attitude that against the background of a living Buddhist tradition, determines our direction, leads us on the way to the depths, and thereby transforms our lives. Only in this way will we, through ever widening experience, gain insight into the nature of reality, in order finally to attain to that perfection of understanding that is Transcendent Wisdom (*prajñāpāramitā*).

3 | *The Role of Morality in the Maturing of the Human Personality*

Moral and ethical behavior ought to be the natural expression of religious experience and true human fellow-feeling. But it should never be made the starting point of a religious view of the world, otherwise it becomes something artificially superimposed or something compulsorily induced. It is true that religions have often taken the view that human beings can only be led to adopt socially acceptable behavior through fear and terror. As a result, many people behaved in a "religiously adequate" manner for fear of "divine punishment" if they failed, or else because they hoped for a reward for their obedience, if not in this world, then at least in heaven after death.

But fear and terror are no means of awakening genuine religiosity or truly ethical and moral behavior in a person. However, ideas that are incalcated into us or that we create for ourselves often have a long-lasting effect on our feelings, thoughts, and actions, and thus on our entire development of character. If someone gets involved in fearful thoughts of hell, he will become more and more afraid, and so adhere to a compulsive, dogma-ruled code of behavior. If, on the other hand, he develops joyful moods such as love, compassion, sympathetic joy, he will be more and more filled with inner happiness and will develop through human fellow-feeling into a personality that is free and at the same time socially responsible.

The Buddha's teaching had from the very beginning only one purpose: to take away the suffering from all sentient beings and make them happy, joyous, and free. Therefore whatever terrifies people, enchains them, frightens them, and binds them to suffering is in conflict with the Dharma of the Exalted One.

It is not the task of religion to proclaim dogmatically specific moral views and ethical demands. The religious sense, rather, is an inborn psychic directedness in mankind, a kind of spiritual centrifugal force that counteracts and largely counterbalances the centripetal tendencies of natural egoism. Thus religion—just like life—has its meaning within itself. It is a spiritual life-form, an individual intensification of consciousness on a supraindividual or even cosmic basis, because its nature is to raise the individual out of his isolation and turn him into a social and finally a cosmic being. In the course of this process of maturation and development, the human being expands into an individuality whose ethical actions are the natural expression of his feeling and thinking, free of all compulsion.

As already remarked, the equation of religion with morality was the most fateful of humanity's mistakes, and judgments such as "good" and "bad" have nothing to do with religion as such. And so the ethic of Buddhism has no injunctions beginning "You must" or "Thou shalt." Each person is regarded as an individual according to the degree of maturity in his insight and spiritual development, and treated as fully responsible accordingly.

Buddhist psychology teaches us that an individual's disposition has three tendencies: that of desiring, that of rejecting (or resisting), and that which is free from both extremes. But desire (like aversion) belongs to the sphere of the instinctive and the idiosyncrasies, and is therefore not subject to free will. Both desire and aversion are expressions of a state of bondage, and are in contrast to the third tendency, which is a state of freedom. Bondage implies that a power is at work and that at the same time there is something that hampers it, so that a relation of tension arises between two systems that are polar opposites. One of these systems is that of the "ego complex," while the other represents the complexity of that which we call "the world."

The attempt to balance this tension that manifests as desire takes one of two forms: either to incorporate parts of the one system in the other, or else to destroy the satisfaction of opposing forces, that is to say, to repulse the forces of the one system by those of the other, or to overcome them by a counterattack. But both these attempts are condemned in advance to failure. Every thrust produces an equally strong counterthrust, every antipathy produces antipathy in return, while every counterpressure produces increased resistance. Analogically, in another phase, we find that desire increases in proportion as we given in to it. Every act of satisfaction is the germ (the continuing cause) of new desire. This works like the suction of a vacuum, and can only be got rid of by the removal of the cause, that is, the removal of the vacuum itself. But if this is as unlimited as the nonvacuum facing it, then the tension cannot be abolished by attempting a balance.

The ego is just such a limitless vacuum, if it is conceived as an independent entity, because in this form it is an abstraction from all that perceptibly exists: something quite exceptional, an ideal vacuum, an illusion. The suction activity of the vacuum expresses itself both in desire and in its reverse—in opposition to everything that opposes the satisfaction of that desire. But resistance leads to an "eddy" in the suction stream, which becomes stronger and more obstructive as the power of suction becomes more intense. But since the illusion consists precisely in the belief in the imaginary "I" as an "absolute," any compromise is foredoomed to failure, and so in this case we can really speak of a "limitless vacuum" as mentioned above. The impossibility of resolving the tension, the complete discrepancy between the subjective will and the objective data, the disharmony between idea and reality—this constitutes what we call "suffering."

The overcoming of this disharmony and these idiosyncrasies or the loosing of the above-mentioned "bondage"—in short, the release to a state of inner freedom—does not come about by fighting against the will, but by the abolition of the vacuum, that is, through the destruction of the illusion of an eternal, unchanging ego or self. In other words, all the suffering of this world arises from a wrong attitude. The world is neither good nor bad. It is only the relation of our ego to it that makes it seem the one or the other.

Whereas the religions of the past mainly demanded from their followers the blind acceptance of unproven articles of faith, the Buddha did not wish to have any blind followers who carried out his instructions without question, without knowing the reason or necessity for them. For him, the value of human thinking lay not in the external result achieved, but solely in the motive of action, that is, in the direction and attitude of consciousness from which the corresponding impulse took its origin. As he declared in his famous words to the Kālāmas,* he wanted his followers to accept the truth of the Dharma he preached to them by their own insight, and not because of their faith in the superiority of his wisdom or his person. The only faith he expected from his pupils was faith in

---

**Aṅguttara Nikāya* 3.66.

their own inner powers. For this reason he put *samyag-dṛṣṭi* (perfect view and insight, or the realization of the Four Noble Truths) at the beginning of his Noble Eightfold Path. It is only through the mental attitude growing out of this realization that the perfect decision that embraces the whole person can ripen, as a result of which our entire human personality undergoes a change in thought, word, and deed, which eventually, through thorough introversion and absorption, leads to perfect enlightenment.

Desire and aversion or, in the usual Buddhist terminology, greed (*lobha*) and hatred (*doṣa*) are here recognized as the principal obstacles on the path. The mind must free itself from these hampering factors by developing helpful powers to counteract them. These are generosity (*dāna*) and love (*maitrī*, Pali *mettā*), which are the precise equivalents of nongreed and nonhatred.

If a person has once realized this deep within, in heart and mind, and if that person has only the one wish remaining, to gain enlightenment for the sake of all beings, then what is "wholesome" (*kuśala*, Pali *kusala*) and "unwholesome" (*akuśala*) will become obvious of its own accord. A truth-seeker will not lie, and one who has the well-being of all beings at heart will avoid slander and harsh speech as well as all vain and foolish chatter.

This rejection of negative forms of behavior has a positively helpful effect for him and for all beings. Thus, according to *Aṅguttara Nikāya* 4.198 (= *Dīgha Nikāya* 1.1.9), "He speaks the truth, is devoted to the truth, trustworthy, dependable. He never consciously speaks a lie either to his own advantage or to the advantage of another or to any advantage, whatever this may be. What he has heard here, he does not repeat elsewhere to cause dissension, but he reconciles those who are at variance and encourages those who are united. Rejoicing in peace, he delights in peace and uses words to bring about peace. Abandoning harsh speech, he refrains from it. He speaks words that are gentle and pleasing to the ear, calming, loving, reaching the heart, urbane, pleasing, and attractive to the multitude. Avoiding idle chatter, he speaks at the right time, what is correct and to the point, of Dhamma and Discipline. He is a speaker whose words are to be treasured, seasonable, reasoned, well-defined, and connected with the goal. This is what is called perfect speech."

The next step on the Noble Eightfold Path, perfect action (*samyak-karmānta*, Pali *sammā kammanta*), is also first expressed negatively as a refraining from killing and stealing and from sexual obsession. But such action and behavior as this, too, can only be called "perfect" (*samyak*) when it arises not from a discipline due to social pressure or adopted for egoistic reasons, but from an attitude that has inwardly matured on the basis of perfect insight, and that harmoniously corresponds to the perfect decision taken as a consequence of this experience. Only then will we be able "without stick or sword (without the application of external force or compulsion), scrupulous and compassionate, to be concerned for the welfare of all beings."*

That such a person cannot choose any profession or follow any occupation that is harmful to the well-being of other beings is obvious. Thus he cannot adopt the profession of arms or deal in arms, living beings, meat, intoxicating liquor and dangerous poisons (as, for instance, drugs), or take employment involving killing, torturing, deception, betrayal, deviousness, usury, bribery, or soothsaying: after such a decisive change in his personality this would not be possible for him. In this way he perfects his way of life, which in the eyes of others appears as a life of purity, of justice, and of action for the community. It proves wholesome for himself as well as for others, is good for both physical and mental well-being, and is placed entirely at the service of all beings, with no need either for the enticements of a creator god with promises of heavenly reward or for threats of hellish punishments.

If a person has developed thus far on the strength of an inner experience, anything that might hinder him on his way or would not be wholesome for him is scarcely likely to arise in his mind. If, on account of old habits, such a thing should once arise, he will reject it and consciously develop and cultivate the positive, wholesome powers that will restore him to harmony with himself and his surroundings. In this way he develops and cultivates those seven factors that, in their complexity and interrelatedness, prepare the way for the breakthrough to enlightenment. These "seven factors of enlightenment" (*sapta-sambodhyaṅga*, Pali *satta sambojjhaṅga*) are (1) mindfulness† (*smṛti*, Pali *sati*), (2) investigation of truth (*dharmavicaya*, Pali *dhammavicaya*), (3) heroic commitment and energy (*vīrya*, Pali *viriya*), (4) inspiration and enthusiasm (*prīti*, Pali *pīti*), (5) inner freedom and calm happiness (*praśrabdhi*,

---

**Dīgha Nikāya* 1.1.8

†*Vergegenwärtigung in klarer Bewusstheit*, lit. "presence of mind with clear awareness."—Trans.

Pali *passaddhi*), (6) deepening and integration (Skt., Pali *samādhi*), and (7) boundless openness toward all beings, which at the same time implies equanimity toward whatever happens to oneself (*upekṣā, Pali upekkhā*).

Through continual labor on himself and the cultivation of the seven factors of enlightenment he will one day be able to complete the seventh step of the Noble Eightfold Path, complete presence of mind (*samyak-smṛti,* Pali *sammā-sati*). Through the clear, fully conscious presence of mind we directly observe the dynamic processes within the bodily sphere, of feelings, of mind and mind-objects. And this deepening of experience derived from direct observation leads to a further speeding up of the transformation of our personality, leading in turn to *samyak-samādhi,* the consolidation and intensification of consciousness itself, that is, to a transformation of consciousness in which the tension between subject and object created by conceptual discrimination is resolved by the integrating power of pure experience. We call this experience "pure" because it is not reflected or colored either through the medium of thought or through any preconceived notions, and is thus free from illusion and its companion states, desire and aversion or attraction and repulsion. When this experience is profound enough to penetrate our entire consciousness down to our deepest roots (*saṃskāras,* Pali *saṅkhāras*), thus revealing our most basic motivation (Skt., Pali *hetu*), then *nirvāṇa* is attained.

But even if such an experience is of lesser intensity and only exercises a limited and temporary influence on our mind, it will still help to broaden our horizon, to strengthen our confidence, deepen our insight, weaken our prejudices, and purify our efforts.

Let us briefly recapitulate. The first step on the path to the highest understanding, that is, the way to perfect enlightenment, consists of an earnest seeking after truth and in the unprejudiced recognition of the laws of life, in so far as they exist within the range of normal human experience. This is the meaning of *samyag-dṛṣṭi,* as the first step on the Noble Eightfold Path. It is significant of the mental attitude of Buddhism that it regards recognition and insight as the first step on the path to liberation, and not the following of a moral law dictated by tradition or laid down in religious commandments. For the Buddhist, morality is the practical expression of his level of understanding, for if he only followed certain rules of moral behavior out of fear of punishment or in the hope of reward, his so-called morality would be lacking in any ethical basis.

From the Buddhist point of view, morality is not the cause but the effect of our mental attitude. Harmony between this attitude and our actions, that is, inner truthfulness, is the real meaning of *śīla* (Pali *sīla*), the literal translation of which is "practice." For this reason, *samādhi*—inner integration and wholeness—is not possible without *śīla*, because concentration and inner unity cannot be achieved without harmony. And just as *śīla* is the result of harmony between our convictions and our actions, so too wisdom (*prajñā*, Pali *paññā*) arises from the harmony between our mind and the laws of reality, and *samādhi* from the harmony between our feelings, knowledge, and volitions, and is thus the mutual attunement of all our creative powers in the experience of a higher reality.

In his enlightenment experience the Buddha had recognized the three root causes (*hetu*) that bind us over and over again to sorrow-laden existences, and which are really nothing but the three manifestations of ignorance (*avidyā*, Pali *avijjā*), for whose overcoming the entire structure of the Buddhist doctrine was erected. The conquest of the three unhealthy roots—greed, hatred, and delusion—comes about by means of nongreed, nonhatred, and nondelusion, bringing with it a transvaluation of all values, whereby nongreed is equated with inner freedom, nonhatred with sympathy, and nondelusion with insight and knowledge.

This method of expressing positive goals and ideas through negative terms shows Buddhism's sense of reality. Positive concepts exist in order to make something graspable or to delimit it. If we say something is green, this excludes all colors *except* green, whereas if we say something is not green, then this admits all colors except green. The reality of our experience knows no limits and boundaries, since everything is in a flux. Thus, if our aim is to remove that which is the opposite, namely delusion—synonymous with "unknowing"—then only negative concepts will suffice, because it is not a question of something new or unprecedented that is opposed to reality. The point is rather to remove that which hinders our understanding of reality. People who cannot see what is gained thereby may regard this as a purely negative operation. But is not everything truly creative really only the overcoming of our restrictions, and could we not really define genius in a sense, as Dahlke once put it, as "preserved ingeniousness" [*erhaltene Unbefangenheit*]?

The wise man, the saint, and above all the enlightened person is one who has broken down all barriers within, has gotten rid of all restrictions, and has thus broken through to the realm of the creative. He is himself the most perfect expression of his own activity, who makes and unmakes himself—the person who is achieving self-liberation by making and unmaking. He has thus become a living focus of the reality that extends far beyond his individual boundaries. While those who have not yet reached this purity of spirit are bound by their own actions, the saint liberates himself in his work. He is "beyond good and evil"—quite apart from the relativity of these concepts, the values of which change at every spiritual step on the Buddhist path, so that one could almost say that the one has its value by the absence of the other, and that after the overcoming of ignorance all oppositions are neutralized. And so, for the perfected one, what in others would be a lack is an honor. Conversely, all the qualities that are normally described as "good" are for the Perfected One the only possible ones.

It thus becomes clear that a perfected one can never become totally passive, although he does neither good nor bad, both of which would be in his power. He has not eradicated the "bad" human qualities in himself, so that only the "good" ones remain, which now, owing to the lack of opposing forces, are no longer considered or termed "good." It is rather that his attitude has become different, because the usual prejudices born of ignorance have dropped away, and therefore those obstacles that count in the Buddhist sense as "unwholesome" no longer exist.

Thus he is in the truest sense "whole," "complete," "perfect," at one with himself, in other words, "healthy." He has overcome the disease of that split caused by the ego-illusion, which is continually at odds with reality and is the cause of "good" and "bad." And for that very reason he is concerned not to deny any single vital quality, but rather to remove the imbalance between existing forces: by this restoration of the balance nothing will be destroyed and nothing new created. If we have an empty balance whose scales are not aligned, we can correct this fault by altering the center of gravity on the beam and not by increasing the load in the higher scale, and so likewise the disharmony in the human psyche must be cured by shifting the center of gravity from "ego" to "nonego."

In this context we can understand the constant use in Buddhism of the terms "wholesome" and "unwholesome" (*kuśala, akuśala*), because "good" and "bad" do not correspond to the Buddhist standpoint any more than do "moral" and "immoral." Therefore the Buddhist can no more accept the idea of sin than of a God who forbids or prescribes things, and against whose commandments one can "sin." For the Buddhist there is only error, unknowing, blindness, and all the kinds of thought and action resulting from this are calamitous above all for the doer. Accordingly, the effect of an action or thought is considered "wholesome" or "unwholesome" to the extent that they do or do not correspond with reality, in accordance with one's understanding or nonunderstanding of this reality.

This makes it clear that neither the overcoming of desire nor that of hatred is sufficient for the attainment of complete liberation. The conquest of desire leads at best to extreme frugality and a simple ascetic way of life. The overcoming of hatred leads to tolerance or, in a positive sense, love of one's neighbor. But the easily satisfied is no more perfect than the compassionate, however much these may stand out among ordinary people. It is only understanding, the casting off of illusion and spiritual limitation, the standing above oneself, that gives desirelessness and neighborly love their real meaning and makes them into attributes of the Perfected One.

Just as desire and aversion or hatred are the two opposing manifestations of ignorance, which condition each other like the positive and negative poles of a magnet, the one attracting and the other repelling, so too freedom from desire and sympathy are the negative and positive poles of the overcoming of the ego-illusion, or the necessary effect of dawning recognition of that reality in which there is no further room for an "I" or, therefore, for egoism, whether in its desiring or in its hating and rejecting form.

But did not the Buddha require asceticism as an inescapable condition for his path to enlightenment? Before we can enter into this question, we must first clarify the question of what constitutes "asceticism" and "enlightenment." *Asceticism* takes many forms, from the extremest types of self-torture to the sublimest forms of self-discipline. The common factor in all these is rejection, restraint, refraining from enjoyments and comforts, and the denial of wishes and inclinations. Indian history shows that asceticism has been practiced for all sorts of different reasons. But if the goal of such asceticism is enlightenment, we can only decide whether this is the proper means of reaching that goal when we know what essentially constitutes enlightenment.

Enlightenment—if we start from the word itself—obviously means the overcoming and dispelling of darkness. Since in our particular case the ideas of light and darkness are applied to our consciousness and our spiritual capacities, enlightenment can be equated with the abolition of all those obstacles that darken the light of knowledge or block its path. In this connection, it is a matter of indifference whether we consider that this light comes from without to fill us, or whether the light is a quality immanent in our own mind. The only important thing is that we recognize the *nature* of the obstacles and find out the method to get rid of them.

As we have seen, the Buddha recognized as obstacles greed, hatred, and ignorance or ego-illusion. Accordingly, enlightenment is gained by overcoming these three obstacles. Greed and hatred are, as we also saw, the emotional extremes of ego-attachment in the form of desire and rejection, greed being unbridled attraction, and hatred its reversal into unbridled animosity.

The reason why we desire one thing and detest another lies in our habit of relating all things to ourselves, that is, to an "ego" thought of as an eternal quantity that remains constantly the same. Thus in our blindness and egocentricity it is impossible for us to see things impartially and objectively—and this is the cause of all our illusions. Greed, hatred, and illusion can thus be reduced to a common denominator—that of the illusion of the isolation of our falsely conceived ego from all other happenings and existences. According to the Buddha's teaching, just this is the cause for the arising of our spiritual blindness and thus of our suffering.

The cure consists in the radical removal of the illusion of a separate "I" and its emotional counterpart, egoism. But although we may intellectually grasp the nature of the illusion, we are still a long way from freeing ourselves emotionally from it, because it has deep roots in our subconscious and has become a component part of our inner nature. We therefore have to trace back the course of development that leads from the symptoms to their origin, that is to say, to their true cause. If in addition we restrict our desires more and more, we have less and less cause to be caught up in anything, or to feel resentment against anything that might interfere with our wishes. To the extent that we are successful in this, the ego-illusion will lose its power over us, because in the moment of letting go we experience a new freedom and a new peace, through which the boundlessness of our nature is revealed to us through an experience that goes far beyond any purely intellectual conviction.

It is true that insights gained by thought can help us to a certain extent, but they can no more bring about a proper cure than can the mere reading or understanding of a medical prescription. We can only be cured by following the doctor's advice and taking the medicine regularly. And so, if we have come to the conviction that through a reduction in our wishes many of the principal hindrances on the way to enlightenment can be removed, then we ought to put this insight into practice. And it is here that the various forms of self-denial and self-discipline characteristic of asceticism can be practiced.

If we have a lofty and noble aim in view, we are ready to make sacrifices for it. For the Buddhist, enlightenment is the only goal worth striving for, and for which every sacrifice is worth while. Therefore a Buddhist is prepared to give up the lesser for the sake of the greater, and in so doing acts wisely. But he would be a fool to give up that which he knows, possesses, and treasures for something of doubtful value. Therefore any kind of asceticism for its own sake is valueless: It only gains a meaning when employed in appropriate fashion for a clearly defined goal. But then the means employed must correspond to the way one has entered upon by being directed to the goal, so that every step confirms the value and rightness of the method chosen.

It is also necessary to employ one's judgment and discrimination in order to come to a correct decision and so to an adequate choice of means, for otherwise asceticism can easily lead to excesses of self-torment, to a vain desire to outdo others, and to a contempt for the world that in its negativity makes impossible from the outset any understanding of the possibilities that this despised world may have to offer. For although the values of this world may seem slight in comparison with those which are aimed at through asceticism, yet they are values, which one should not despise without close examination. After all, the Buddha regarded the experiential value of human existence as being higher than that of all other forms of existence, even those in the heavenly realms!

He therefore condemned all self-torment just as much as the

unbridled satisfaction of sensual desires. Both destroy the bases of physical and mental health, without which spiritual progress is not possible. The Buddha had found this out in his own person. He had practiced the most extreme forms of asceticism to the limit of self-destruction, and had been forced to admit that this did not lead to enlightenment. He recognized that asceticism, like every other extreme of excess, can easily lead to a flight from life and then, like any form of flight, must lead away from the goal. But true asceticism as a disciplinary practice never stands apart from life. It consists in the elimination of all those factors that hinder us in the fulfilling and perfection of our life—the breakthrough to enlightenment. Just as rays of light are concentrated in a lens and thus are so intensified in effect that they immediately set fire to flammable material that otherwise could have been exposed indefinitely to the same rays without danger, in the same way anyone who practices asceticism in the right way can increase the effectiveness of his spiritual powers in that direction. In this way he becomes capable of gaining in the short span of a single life what others are unable to attain in the course of innumerable lives.

However, anyone who makes use of these concentrated powers without proper insight into the nature of his chosen goal will go astray. Enlightenment presupposes the experience of egolessness. But anyone who thinks enlightenment is the result of the mere suppression of all our desires shows that he is still under the sway of an illusory belief in an ego or self; thus he is still trapped in ignorance, so that instead of growing beyond the narrow bounds of his ego, he separates himself from the surrounding world and his fellow beings, and finally ends up in a mental vacuum. Whoever seeks his "own" salvation without regard to his fellow beings may be a virtuous and noteworthy person, but nevertheless he remains an egoist. The narrow and unavoidable intolerance that grows from such an attitude is directly opposed to the marks of enlightenment, which are love, fellow feeling, tolerance, generosity, and selflessness.

But these qualities cannot be gained either by self-tormenting asceticism or by mere learning. Only through love and compassion for all sentient beings can we break through the hard crust of our ego-isolation and overcome the illusion of separateness. It is only when we combine the knowing of the heart with the knowing of the brain that knowledge turns into wisdom, and the rigid self-discipline of asceticism turns into the spiritual harmony of an enlightened one. The question of whether asceticism can lead to enlightenment must, on the basis of the above, receive the following answer: asceticism alone leads nowhere. But when combined with wisdom and compassion it can lead the practicer to the goal of enlightenment and liberation.

The Buddha, who is our model on the Noble Eightfold Path, was a man of the highest spiritual discipline. His teaching stresses the disciplining of the daily routine for both monks and disciples living a worldly life. If today the view is sometimes expressed that all we need to break through to inner freedom is "to be all there," this does not agree with the Buddha's view. For him, slackness and letting oneself go, just like wallowing in sentiment and fantasy, meant that such a person was on the "slippery slope."

Asceticism (from Greek *askésis*) means "practice" and is thus a synonym of the Sanskrit word *śīla* (Pali *sīla*), in the sense of the five moral undertakings that every Buddhist daily renews as a task. He takes them on not because they are the commandments of a deity, but from personal insight. In full personal responsibility he undertakes to strive in thought, word, and deed not to harm life, not to take what is not given, to lead a life of purity, to refrain from lies and harsh speech, and neither to get drunk nor to becloud his consciousness. These five practices are called *pañcaśīla*. A Buddhist living the homeless life undertakes a further five which, like the 250 or so monastic rules, are secondary in character.

What is the nature of the "insight" that leads a Buddhist to take on these five *śīlas*? Primarily, it is the sense of responsibility arising from the fact that he identifies with all sentient beings or, as the texts put it, "equates himself with them." He has come to realize that through acts, words, and thoughts that do not correspond to these rules he harms other beings. Through this he falls into a state of disharmony with the world about him, and as a reaction will himself experience suffering, and his path to enlightenment will be blocked. Therefore an action that is contrary to the *śīlas* is termed "unwholesome" (*akuśala*), because it does serious harm not only to others, but also to oneself, since the five *skandhas** (Pali *khandhas*) that constantly reshape our personality

*The *skandhas*, also called "elements of existence" or "aggregates of clinging," are the components out of which the physical and mental existence of a human being is continually made and remade. They are selectively effective, assimilatory forces in the five realms of corporeality, feelings, perceptions and thought processes, instinctive and volitional tendencies, and consciousness.

in their continuous transformation are influenced in an unwholesome way.

In order to practice the *śīlas* in the proper way, we need to have insight into the conditional nature of our humanity, and to recognize that there is no isolated existence in the universe, but that everything is interwoven in a play of endless mutual relationships, expressed in *pratītya-samutpāda* or dependent origination. It is from this knowing about our involvement in endless, universal interrelationships that there grows and ripens within us the feeling of solidarity with all living beings, and we come to recognize our responsibility toward the whole. It is the merit of the Mahāyāna to have brought about an awareness of these relationships.

In the accounts of some early Buddhist schools we are wonderfully moved by the attitudes and examples of an ideal moral way of life. But these are without any real value if they are based on an ethic that is practiced for its own sake. Of course we can say, "Do good!" or "Lead a moral life!" or "Do this and not that!"; but even if one were to practice all the virtues in the world without knowing why, it would be better to abandon such virtue, because it often brings more sorrow than happiness, besides easily encouraging a feeling of pride that one is better than other people. Only the person who avoids certain actions and performs others from a feeling of conscious responsibility toward all that lives is one who really acts in an ethically wholesome manner. Only he can liberate himself from the fetters of egocentric feeling and sensation (*vedanā*) and arouse in himself that all-embracing compassion that enables him to feel inward sympathy with all that lives. The unity of all life can never be felt more deeply than in sharing the joy and sorrow, happiness and suffering of others. Out of this there develops the urge to give, and finally to surrender one's own ego in self-sacrifice to all beings on the path of bodhisattvahood.

We are living in a time of vast changes, in a time in which the science created by humanity threatens to destroy humankind. We have come to this point by releasing forces that increasingly escape our control. And so man, under the sway of the intellect that produced this knowledge, is becoming a part of the very mechanism that destroys the individual by extinguishing the last traces of the human and the divine—precisely that which makes us human beings. For being human combines the uniqueness and singularity of the individual with something numinous that lifts that individual out of his solitariness and at the same time conveys to him the experience of being interwoven with the entire universe. The Buddha taught that this "divine" that transcends our normal selves can be realized by the awakening of four unlimited meditative states (*brahamavihāras* "divine abidings," or *appamaññas* "boundless states"), that is, love (*maitrī*, Pali *mettā*), pity or compassion (*karuṇā*), sympathetic joy (*muditā*), and a boundless turning to all beings without distinction, from which evolves a state of equanimity regarding whatever happens to oneself (*upekṣā*, Pali *upekkhā*).

The first of these "divine abidings," *maitrī*, is the key that frees us from the prison of selfhood and opens up for us the depths of space. In spite of all philological pedantry and learned controversies, *maitrī* is more than "friendship," "benevolence," "kindness," "friendliness," or "goodwill." It has only one equivalent that, in spite of its ambiguity, alone gets to the heart of the matter: it is self-sacrificing *love* in its highest and purest sense.

The fact that love has innumerable gradations and can occur in innumerable different combinations does not alter its essential nature. Love is like a flame that burns up all impurity and transforms it into warmth and light. Anyone who disputes the warmth of the *maitrī* extolled by the Buddha has not understood the meaning of either Buddhism or love. Even when love is an accompaniment of sexual desire, this does not degrade love, but lifts sexuality from the level of an animal function to the height of a spiritual experience. Just as Christianity did not hesitate to translate the Greek *agape* as "love" and to allot the highest place to this—despite all the secondary meaings and associations it calls up—so too Buddhists have no reason to be frightened of the word "love" and to hide timorously behind meaningless moral concepts or abstract ethical principles.

Rather, we should realize that a person who in private life is incapable of passionate love can certainly not develop true devotion on a higher spiritual plane or achieve real self-sacrifice. Let us then be on our guard against those false prophets of "clinical purity," germ-free morality, and abstinence that is hostile to life, and let us give all our warmth of heart, even the fervor of our deepest love, to our fellow human beings without bargaining or judging or expecting to get "ours" back again, precisely on account of that great love that the Exalted One called "liberation of heart and mind" (Pali *cetovimutti*), which is the purest flame of our being, in which all selfishness is burnt up.

Thus the Buddha twenty-five hundred years ago—five hundred years before the apostle Paul's famous encomium of love (1 Cor. 13)—extolled love as that faculty that far more than all other lofty and loftiest religious and ethical deeds, is capable of softening the hardened ego-structure or the ego-delusion, in order thereby to effect the disengagement of the *upadhis** and so open the way to liberation and enlightenment. And so he declared:

> Monks, whatever wholesomely effective means one may undertake in this life† with a view to a good rebirth, they are all not worth one sixteenth part of that love that is liberation of the heart (and mind); this love alone, which is liberation of the heart (and mind), includes them all in itself and shines and glows and flashes forth.
> And, monks, just as the radiance of all the stars is not worth one sixteenth part of the moon's radiance, but the moon's radiance includes them all in itself and shines and glows and flashes forth, so too, monks, such means are not worth one sixteenth part of that love that is liberation of the heart; this love alone includes them all in itself and shines and glows and flashes forth.
> And just as, monks, in the last month of the rainy season, in the autumn, the sun rises in the clear and cloudless sky, driving away all darkness from the heavens and shines and glows and flashes forth, so too, monks, such means are not worth one sixteenth part of that love that is liberation of the heart; this love alone includes them in itself and shines and glows and flashes forth.
> And just as, monks, in the night toward morning the morning star shines and glows and flashes forth, whatever wholesomely effective means one may undertake in this life with a view to a good rebirth are not worth one sixteenth part of that love that is liberation of the heart; this love alone, which is liberation of the heart, includes them all in itself and shines and glows and flashes forth.

He went on:

> Whoever causes love to grow
> Boundlessly, with mind intent,

**Upadhi* = "substrate, addition." The term means the complex consisting of the five *skandhas*, sensuality (*kāma*), the defilements (*kleśa*, Pali *kilesa*: greed, hatred, delusion, pride, prejudice, doubt, obstinacy, agitation, shamelessness, and lack of conscience), together with karma (Pali *kamma*), the force that leads to rebirth—in other words, the elements that bring about the forms of human existence.

†*Opadhika* = related to *upadhi*. The wholesomely effective means are *opadhika*, because they cannot lead beyond the realm of *saṃsāra* and so of impermanence (Pali *anicca*), but can lead to a good rebirth.

Shall see the substrates disappear
And the fetters wearing thin.

But though whoever pure of heart
Feels love towards a single being
Does well—that Noble's gain
Who loves all beings is limitless.
(*Itivuttaka* 27)

And in another place he says:

> Therefore, monks, you should learn thus: that love that is the liberation of the heart and the mind, we will produce in ourselves, increase it, further it and make it wholly ours, practice it, perfect it more and more, and employ it to perfection.

But the development of such love that embraces equally all beings cannot be achieved without the experience of suffering. Whoever equates *priya** (Pali *piya*) and *maitrī* (Pali *mettā*)—under that most miserable and egoistic of excuses: "whoever loves nothing suffers nothing"—in order to escape from suffering deprives himself of the noblest fruit of human life. For out of the experience of suffering of a loving heart that mature understanding, that highest wisdom grows that is embodied in the figure of Prajñāpāramitā.

The way to the development of *maitrī* regularly begins with loving, embracing, opening devotion to *one* being, not in order to possess that being, to make it subject to oneself or to shape it according to one's own image, but to set it free and stimulate it to unfold the slumbering powers within. For *maitrī* never seeks its own. The lover steps back and turns himself into a springboard.

Through such devoted attention, in *maitrī*, to one being, the loving person increasingly develops love for all beings. Just as, in Hermann Hesse's *Siddhartha*, Govinda, when moved by love, finds his friend's forehead transparent, so that he can see the interpenetration and unity of all life—an egoless becoming in constant transformation—so through our love for one being *maitrī* brings us to a love for all that lives, because through it we become aware of the unity of being and learn to break down all barriers. For it is in this act of seeing and knowing that what the Buddha called *attānam upamaṃ katvā* ("likening others to oneself") occurs. In

**Priya* = whatever is dear and pleasant to one.

this total identification *maitrī* turns into *mahākaruṇā* and *muditā*, the great compassion and sympathetic joy, self-forgetfulness in the sharing of the sorrows and joys of other beings.

It was the Mahāyāna that allotted the central position in Buddhist ethics to compassion (*karuṇā*) paired with wisdom (*prajñā*), seeing the essential features of every enlightened being in the highest development and union of these two. For wisdom without compassion can easily lead into a realm where everything becomes rigid with cold, while compassion without wisdom always involves the danger of lapsing into mere sentiment and getting involved in activities that regularly and senselessly waste one's energy.

If we seriously want to help other beings, we must not be carried away by our feelings. Rather, we must first learn to understand those beings and their situation, and investigate their resources and reserves of strength. Only then can we be of use to them in seeking a path that is adequate to their needs. But such help must never lead to depriving others of personal responsibility and achievement. We can point out ways, but we cannot tread them for others. Love and true compassion will always try to avert disasters from others, but without hindering or hampering the others' own life and experience.

Love and sympathy for our fellow human beings can and should give others on the early stages of the path the strength to carry on consistently, because they feel supported and encouraged through our love and through our positive belief in their inherent abilities. However, wisdom must avoid renewing all inconvenient obstacles from their path, and must ensure that they do not avoid conflicts but learn to pass through them, also that they do not develop or encourage pride, vanity, egocentricity, or even the feeling of being something special, instead of cutting these things down; they must also learn, in the face of seeming injustices, to question their own position instead of accusing others or making them responsible.

It was the Mahāyāna that very early developed symbolic images in which the highest embodiment of *maitrī* and *mahākaruṇā* manifested, as in the figures of Tārā, Avalokiteśvara, and the future buddha Maitreya. The latter, who as the great lover prepares to descend into this world in order to show us the way of egoless and therefore karma-free action, is the Pole Star in the darkness of our time. May his call reach the hearts of humanity, for it is there alone that the place of renewal of the world and the reembodiment of an Enlightened One is to be found!

4 | *The Bodhisattva Ideal: A Light in the Darkness of Our Time*

The difference between an ideal and a dogma is that an ideal makes no claim to exclusivity. It furthers and encourages the liberty of individual decision, and therefore—unlike a dogma—needs no justification through historical documents or logical proofs. Its immediate force of conviction arises from its indwelling power of renewed inspiration and creative shaping of the future. It is this that gives it its value in and for the present.

So too the bodhisattva ideal, which has largely shaped Buddhist life, thought, and action for more than two thousand years, needs no justification through scholasticism, dogmatism, or religious history, for it is the expression of an inner attitude that has repeatedly demonstrated its power of transformation, which has inspired the individual to the realization of that lofty goal to which the Buddha, by his own example, has pointed the way for us.

This way is neither simple nor easy. Anyone who starts on it develops a feeling of responsibility that extends to ever wider circles, and he is carried ever more and more out of the security of the small and easily surveyed world of personal joy and sorrow into an activity that demands the commitment of all his powers for the benefit of all beings. There is no room here for a quietist retreat from the world. Here, it is a matter of actively *overcoming* the world, not a "getting out of the world" but a "going right through and beyond the world." But those who tread this path feel richly rewarded by the inward happiness they feel from the burgeoning knowledge of being one with all that lives. And so the bodhisattva ideal appeals today, as always, to the deepest human feelings in our hearts. It fills us with the fire of devotion to a great goal for which one is glad to make any sacrifice, without feeling that it *is* a sacrifice.

As long as the Buddha was present among his disciples as the living embodiment of this ideal, there was no need to evolve theories or develop specific ideas and opinions about the nature of bodhisattvahood. But after the passing of the Exalted One, his pupils realized fully for the first time the Buddha's real greatness, just as we can only recognize the size of a mountain when we regard it from a certain distance. And so, at a certain distance of time, the image of the Buddha became ever clearer in the hearts of his followers. It took more and more perfect shape till he was finally recognized for what he had always been: the one who had in exemplary fashion shown the way that every true disciple has to go, the way of bodhisattvahood in the service of all beings, that leads to the lofty goal—the goal of perfect enlightenment, which is the great awakening.

Thus the bodhisattva ideal, in spite of its relatively late verbal formulation, is not some "invention" of the centuries after the Buddha's *parinirvāṇa*, but is one of the basic ideas of early Buddhism. This is clear through the Jātakas, which belong to the oldest Buddhist tradition, and whose enormous influence on the whole of Buddhist culture over a period of thousands of years in the whole of Asia is unmistakable, in literature, painting, and sculpture in South, Central, and East Asia. We need only mention as examples the frescoes and sculptures of Ajanta and the marvelous reliefs of the Borobudur.

There is no need for any Buddhist to believe in these stories of rebirths, even though the Buddha spoke in his discourses about his former lives. Here too, Buddhism is not dogmatic. But these tales make vividly clear to everyone the ideal that reveals the essential basis of the Dharma: selflessness, readiness to sacrifice oneself from love and compassion, and the rejection of self-interest for the benefit of others. It was this path that the Buddha, as a living example, displayed, and that he revealed to his disciples through doctrinal discourses and meditation instructions.

Already on Indian soil, during the first few centuries after the Buddha's time, there were differences of evaluation and interpretation of certain parts of his teaching, due to the various temperaments and the more introvert or extrovert characters of his followers. As a result, different ideals developed and led to the controversy between the *arahat* and the bodhisattva ideals. A later development led to the belief that the Theravāda school, which had been isolated in Ceylon for centuries, was committed (and with it the entire Pali tradition) to the *arahat* ideal just like the eighteen long-vanished "Hīnayāna" schools. Yet it is precisely in the Pali tradition that we find one of the oldest bodhisattva vows:

> Sīla-nekkhamma-paññādiṃ
> pūretvā sabba-pāramiṃ
> pārami-sikkhanaṃ patvā
> Buddho hessam anuttaro.*
>
> Through the
> accomplishment of all
> perfections:
> morality, renunciation,
> wisdom, and the rest
> (i.e., generosity, energy,
> patience, truthfulness,
> determination, loving-
> kindness and equanimity),
> and through their highest
> realization,
> may I attain to supreme
> Buddhahood.

This bodhisattva vow shows that the Theravāda school cannot simply be counted as part of the Hīnayāna: when the ideological distinction between Hīnayāna and Mahāyāna arose, this school had long since disappeared from the Indian mainland, apart from a small detached group near Amarāvatī in the south. In this context it should also be noted that the value of the Pali tradition is recognized by *all* Buddhist schools. It is undoubtedly one of the oldest traditions, and because of its isolation in Ceylon it has preserved the most complete canon of any school. It would, however, be wrong to claim that this canon represents "the only authentic word of the Buddha" and that Pali is the Buddha's language. The Buddha spoke Māgadhī, a north Indian language, and translations into Sanskrit and Pali only followed later, at first orally, and later, after revision at various councils, in written form (from about 90 B.C.E.).

Thus the canonical collections of the various schools arose and existed side by side. Of most of these collections, only fragments survive, mainly in Tibetan or Chinese translations. The genuine-

*After Anagarika Dharmapala, founder of the Mahā Bodhi Society, who included it in the daily *pūjā* for his monks.

ness of the Pali tradition, and the honesty of its followers, was never doubted by even the staunchest supporters of Mahāyāna Buddhism. But neither the Mahāyānists nor the followers of other schools could accept the claim that the Pali canon was the sole authentic source of the word of the Buddha. It is obvious that other, equally serious disciples of the Exalted One have preserved other aspects of the same teaching. This is proved by the Theravāda tradition itself, which refers to the *sthavira* (elder) Purāṇa's arrival with a following of five hundred monks just as the elders had established the text of the Buddha's discourses at the First Council. When this had all been recited to him and he was asked to agree to it, he remarked that what the elders had fixed was all very well, but he preferred "to remember the Buddha's words just as he had heard them from the Exalted One's own lips." Whereupon he left with his monks.

A similar liberty was also claimed by the sixth patriarch of the Ch'an school, Hui-neng, when he declared: "The *sūtras* and scriptures of Mahāyāna and Hīnayāna and the twelve sections of the canonical scriptures were composed to suit the varying temperaments and needs of different people."

And so those who inclined toward philosophical abstraction tried to reach the goal by the study of the Abhidharma. Others, who were less philosophically minded, preferred the ethic of the *sūtras*, while those who were more concerned with the monastic life turned to the Vinaya. But those who found their greatest inspiration in the person of the Buddha made his life and the perfection of his phenomenal existence the principal subject of their meditations, and looked to the Jātakas as the most perfect expression of their ideal.

From the standpoint of the history of religion, it should be noted that what the various schools later called the "Third Basket"—the Abhidharma Piṭaka—and included in their canonical scriptures is merely a systematic compendium of the doctrine, which was only put together after the Buddha's *parinirvāṇa*. The systematically organized meditations there, with the corresponding psychological definitions and classifications, are the work of scholasticism, which is based, logically and consistently, on the foundations of the teaching as given out by the Buddha.

In the same way, the bodhisattva ideal was not formulated or created by the Buddha himself. This was done by those who adopted the Exalted One's teaching less through the transmitted word than by regarding the Buddha as the living embodiment of the Dharma. Consistently with this, they made the imitation of his earthly life, of his spiritual development, and his self-sacrificing activity the ideal and guiding star of their own lives and strivings. For what could give anyone greater certainty, amid the crossfire of mutually opposed worldviews and opinions, than the example of the Buddha, which one only had to follow? Even if in the course of changing times his words might be variously interpreted, his living example speaks an eternal language, which will be understood at all times as long as human beings inhabit this earth. This explains, for example, the astonishing success of Sir Edwin Arnold's *Light of Asia* (1879), which brought more people to Buddhism than did the philologically accurate translations of the original texts or treatises on the philosophy of religion, however valuable and necessary these might be.

This very fact makes it clear that the figure of the Buddha and the profound symbolism of his life, whether historical or legendary, in which his inner development is related, is of infinitely greater significance for humanity than all the philosophical systems based on his teaching or the abstract classifications of the Abhidharma. For can there be a finer and more profound expression of selflessness, the *anātman* doctrine, of the Four Noble Truths including the Noble Eightfold Path, of dependent origination and of perfect enlightenment and liberation, than in the life of the Buddha, which embraces all the heights and depths of the universe? Was not his whole existence and activity a living expression of what is the kernel of the bodhisattva vow: "Whatever may be the highest perfection of the human spirit, may I realize it for the benefit of all beings"?

Just as an artist chooses as his models the greatest masters in his field, irrespective of whether he will ever be able to reach their perfection, so too whoever seeks spiritual progress must turn to the highest ideal within the bounds of his understanding, and this will spur him on to ever greater efforts and struggles. Nobody can say in advance just where the boundaries lie of one's own creative powers. In fact, it is probable that the intensity of our effort and the power of our devotion to the goal determines where these boundaries lie, so that whoever seeks the highest goal with total commitment of his psychic energy will become imbued with the greatest strength and his limitations will increasingly vanish into the endless distance.

For anyone who has chosen this path, it matters little whether only one Buddha can appear in a particular *kalpa* (world period) or not. He will and must act at all times as if the appearance of the next buddha depended on his personal efforts. Far more important than all speculations about how many buddhas can appear within a *kalpa* is the conception, accepted by all Buddhist schools, of the cosmic periodicity of the appearance of enlightened beings. This means that though the appearance of a *samyak-sambuddha* (Perfectly Enlightened Buddha) is a very rare occurrence, nevertheless the "germ," the potential power and tendency toward the unfolding of the "enlightenment consciousness" (*bodhicitta*), is immanent in the entire universe, and that it therefore lies slumbering in every living being and is capable of being awakened.

If this fundamental principle has once been accepted, then the question of the numerical symbols by which it is expressed becomes of no consequence. Thus, for instance, the schools of Northern Buddhism (although they assume a group of principal buddhas in one *kalpa*, as idealized archetypes and representatives of certain spiritual qualities) do not deny the existence of innumerable other buddhas and bodhisattvas, and they stress the possibility of a breakthrough to enlightenment for *all* beings on the most varied levels of spiritual development. For in a universe which knows neither temporal nor spatial limitations, dogmatic assertions and statistics about possible developments and life forms lose all meaning. Put positively, this means: *The spirit has no other boundaries than those it creates for itself.*

Understood like this, the multitude of buddhas and bodhisattvas in the Mahāyāna is simply an expression of the idea that the highest goal can be realized always and everywhere, and is not dependent on certain temporal constellations, local preconditions, or particular circumstances. It follows that, as far as Buddhism is concerned, miracles in the sense of a challenge to or breach of the law-abiding order of the world do not exist. What we call "miracles" are just unexpected revelations of the reality of our mind. Miracles are not exceptional events in nature, but exceptional states of consciousness. That is why the Buddha called the transformation of our mind "the turn in the innermost seat of consciousness"—that is, from an egocentric to an ego-free attitude—and this was the only miracle deserving of the name.

This miracle occurs when we first become conscious of our

capacity for enlightenment, when for the first time the consciousness of enlightenment seizes hold of us. This flashing forth of the *bodhicitta* gives one's life a new meaning and an unshakeable directedness toward the great goal. This fundamental change in the emotional and spiritual attitude is the only important thing. Compared with this, all attempts to establish "statistically" what percentage of all those who seek the highest goal within a particular period have a chance of success, are nothing but playful speculation, just like the efforts of certain naive "scientific" critics of the bodhisattva ideal who tried to work out the length of time necessary for such a chance to be realized.

The senselessness of such an undertaking was demonstrated already in the *Laṅkāvatāra Sūtra*, in the course of a profound dialogue between the Buddha and Mahāmati, in which the latter, like most modern skeptics, is a little disturbed about the How and When of his liberation and now wants to know what chance a bodhisattva has of reaching *nirvāṇa*. He asks, "Pray, Exalted One, tell us, how do bodhisattvas gain certainty of *nirvāṇa*?" The Lord answered, "Mahāmati, this certainty is not a certainty of numbers or of logic, it is not thought that gains certainty here, but the heart. The bodhisattva's certainty comes with the unfolding of insight, which arises when the hindrances of the passions have been removed, when the obstacles to knowledge have been swept aside, when egolessness has been clearly perceived and patiently accepted."

This last sentence of our quotation should make it quite clear that the bodhisattva path does not differ in a single point from the Noble Eightfold Path of the Buddha, and that there is therefore no room for foolish ideas such as the "conscious retention of the passions," as the followers of the bodhisattva ideal are accused of by their opponents. The cultivation of profound insight through meditation, the conquest of the passions through discipline, the clarification of knowledge through study, the realization of nonselfhood (*nairātmyā*) through selflessness, and enlightenment—these are the pillars on which the bodhisattva ideal reposes.

It is a dangerous half-truth to suppose that one must first help oneself before one can help others. Life shows us again and again that we cannot help ourselves without helping others at the same time, because it is not success or the external visible effect that is of importance, but the motive, the inner attitude, the need and readiness to help others. This readiness alone frees us from the condition of setting ourselves apart from others and from the isolation so engendered (which is such a marked feature of our time) and enables us to grow beyond ourselves.

Whoever has been seized by the bodhisattva ideal will soon find himself compelled by his readiness to help others and to assist them on their way, to teach the path—as far as he himself has at that stage understood it—to others. Here, too, the critics representative of orthodox opinion raise objections, although they ought to be familiar from the Pali canon (*Mahāvagga* 1.23) with the story of Sāriputta's sudden enlightenment through the simple statement of the teaching by Assaji, who himself had only just become a disciple of the Buddha. And is it not the case that someone who is still learning is often a better teacher for those wrestling with beginners' difficulties than someone who believes he knows it all, and so has lost the capacity to take in and assimilate anything new? The person who stands at the beginning is usually very conscious of the limitations of his knowledge, and therefore, in passing it on, limits himself to that which he has clearly understood or has gained by personal experience. Such a person wants to share the joy and happiness so gained with others without conceit or vanity.

Such sharing out of joy, in full consciousness of the limitations of one's own knowledge, is a very different thing from the excessive zeal and missionary fervor of those who want to give the world the "benefit" of their new ideas. Here, the admonition of moderation and restraint is important. We should never forget that we can only serve other beings to an increasing extent if we are working hard on ourselves every moment to integrate body, speech, and thought to form an ever more perfect instrument for serving the well-being of all beings and in order to attain to buddhahood "for the sake of all beings trapped in suffering." For the gaining of this lofty goal, the practice of the *pāramitās,** the "highest perfections," is an

---

**Pāramitā* = "perfection." The lists in the Pali canon and in the Mahāyāna differ. In the Pali canon they are: *dāna, sīla, nekkhamma, paññā, viriya, khanti, sacca, adiṭṭhāna, mettā, upekkhā* (generosity, morality, renunciation, wisdom, energy, patience, truthfulness, determination, loving-kindness, equanimity). The original six *pāramitās* of the Mahāyāna were later increased to ten, corresponding to the steps of the bodhisattva path: *dāna, śīla, kṣanti, vīrya, dhyāna, prajñā* and *upāya, praṇidhāna, bala, jñāna* (generosity, morality, patience, energy, meditation, wisdom and proper use of means, solemn asseveration, strength, and illumined, intuitive wisdom).

indispensable prerequisite on the bodhisattva path. These perfections consist not only in the avoidance of what is evil and unwholesome and the cultivation of what is good and wholesome, but above all in self-sacrificing acts of love and compassion, born of the fires of universal suffering in which the suffering of others are felt with the same intensity as one's own.

A bodhisattva does not cherish the ambition to lecture others continually in words. He wishes to teach, above all, by his own example. And so he pursues his spiritual path without ever forgetting the welfare of his fellow beings, growing in maturity as he approaches his lofty goal, and inspiring others to do likewise. On this path no sacrifice that we make for the sake of other beings is in vain, even if it is not recognized as such, or indeed even if it is misused by those for whose well-being it was made. Every sacrifice, being an act of renunciation, is a victory over ourselves, and therefore an act of liberation. Irrespective of its outward effect, it brings us a step nearer to our goal, and transforms our theoretical understanding of the *anātman* ideal into a living knowledge and certainty born of experience. For the more we free ourselves from our ego and tear down the walls of our self-created prison, the greater will be the brightness and clarity of our being, and the greater the conviction carried by the exemplary life we lead. Only in this way can we help others—more than through works of philanthropy, and more than through pious phrases and religious sermons.

Anyone who thinks he can reach the goal more rapidly by fleeing the world and shutting himself off from all contact with life deprives himself of the opportunity to make sacrifices, to practice self-denial, to give up one's hard-earned gains and reject things one likes, or to keep aloof from what seems to one desirable. World-renunciation is a standpoint adopted by people who personally suffer from life and who are so fixated on their own suffering that they fail to observe the often much greater sufferings of others, and are therefore only concerned with getting rid of their own suffering. Others, however, *see* the suffering of the beings that surround them and feel that suffering with them, and are prepared to accept all pains and difficulties in order to bring solace to those beings.

People in the first group, who only see their own suffering and seek their own liberation from suffering, become caught up and imprisoned in egocentricity and selfish obduracy, which according to the Buddha's teaching is the cause of all suffering, which has to be overcome. If we were to proceed at this point with purely analytical meditation methods, the idea of self-deliverance would narrow the mental field of vision to a single point of egocentric intellectual understanding, which would finally reduce everything that happens in the world to a condition of meaninglessness from which it would seem to dissolve into nothingness. Only when this analytic meditation is complemented by insight into the nature of things that aims at synthesis and integration (or, rather, by the intuitive understanding of the mutually interdependently arising connections between all phenomena) can it lead to spiritual progress.

Accordingly, the meditator has to learn to regard things from a universal standpoint, without bringing in an ego separate from the totality of events, and so in this way to observe the universal interconnectedness of all phenomena. Only when this is achieved does the ego as if spontaneously lose its rigidity and become transparent, without any particular effort being made to destroy it by force. For that would merely strengthen its illusory "reality," just as the denial of its relative existence would only lead to self-deception. For as long as all our actions are directed to self-preservation, and as long as our every thought is devoted to self-interest, all our protests against the existence of an ego are completely meaningless. In the circumstances it is much more truthful and honest to admit that we still possess an ego, or rather that we are possessed by an ego, in the same way as many a thinker is possessed by certain fixed ideas or illusions, and that really we can only hope to be free of it one day.

But if we are to aim at this goal, we must first of all determine our own position, that is to say we must see ourselves in true perspective in relation to the rest of the world. Such a perspective opens out before us when we regard ourselves from the standpoint of an all-transcending universal teaching such as we find, for example, in the Dharma of the Buddha, as well as in the inspiring, exemplary life of the Enlightened One. As long as we look at life from the narrow and limited viewpoint of daily life, it seems meaningless. Yet anyone who penetrates to a universal view of the whole finds out how this whole is mirrored in the mind of an enlightened being, and comes to find a meaning in it. But this understanding of the highest, or transcendent, reality cannot be expressed in human speech, unless with labels like *samyak-*

sambodhi (perfect enlightenment) or *nirvāṇa,* which the Buddha clearly defined as "freedom from greed, hatred, and delusion," in contrast to the Brahmin interpretation, whereby this concept was turned into a vague metaphysical entity.

In Buddhism, the question was never raised as to whether life in itself has a meaning of its own or not: from the point of view of the Dharma this is a meaningless question. The important thing for the practice of the Dharma is that each one of us should give his own life an individual meaning. Just as in the hands of an inspired artist a worthless lump of clay can turn into a priceless work of art, so we too should try similarly to form the existing "clay" of our lives into something of value, instead of bewailing the worthlessness of life. Our life, and the world, have just as much "meaning" as we ascribe to them and put into them.

"Man is just as immortal as his ideal, and just as real as the energy with which he serves it." These words of Count Keyserling point in the right direction. The problems of value and reality depend on our attitude and the creative realization of our ideals, and not on any sort of conceptual "objectivity."

If, therefore, we have elevated the enlightened ones and the goal of enlightenment to our highest ideal, this will become for us an active reality to the precise extent that we follow the example of the enlightened ones on the path of bodhisattvahood, exerting ourselves with might and main. In so doing, we must be aware from the beginning that on this path there is neither a chance to escape nor any way of avoiding or running away from difficulties and suffering. This path demands the full and total commitment of our entire psychic energy, and a readiness to take upon ourselves the suffering of *all* beings. But this acceptance of the sufferings of the world does not mean that we should seek out suffering or glory in it, or adopt it as a kind of penance, as was and is done by certain ascetics in various religions. This is an extreme to be avoided just as much as excessive devotion to our own well-being and entanglement in sensual pleasures.

Here, one thing alone is necessary, that we should learn to identify with all living beings. This attitude not only prevents us from attaching too much importance to our own suffering (which would merely strengthen our self and our self-obsession); it also helps us to overcome egocentricity and to make light of our own suffering in the face of that of others. In this way the Buddha once led the mentally confused and disturbed Kisā-Gotamī, who could not grasp the fact of the death of her only son, to overcome her mental distress by letting her see and experience the fact that death is a universal experience to which all beings are subject. Thus he showed her that she was not alone in her sorrow, and that whoever can take this sorrow into his mind and accept it has already won at least half the battle, if not the whole battle.

When the Buddha proclaimed his teaching of the cessation of suffering, he did not speak of "avoiding suffering." If this had been his aim, he could, according to Buddhist tradition, have chosen the short path to liberation, which lay within the realm of possibility for him at the time of the buddha Dīpaṅkara: he would have spared himself the suffering of innumerable rebirths. But he knew that only the one who has passed through the purifying fire of suffering can gain the highest enlightenment, in order to serve the world. His path was not to flee from suffering but to overcome suffering, to conquer it. That is why he, like the buddhas before him, was called a *jina*, a "victorious one."

He and his predecessors overcame suffering by facing it heroically. For one who is on the way to perfect enlightenment, suffering loses its character of personal distress and no longer concerns itself with worries about one's own private well-being; it becomes more and more universal and essential, including in its purview the nature of all existence. It is in this spirit that the bodhisattva vow is taken by all those who wish to follow the sacred path of the Buddha: "Whatever spiritual gains I may have attained to, may I thereby become an assuager of the sufferings of other sentient beings. The spiritual gains that I have made on all my paths of life by thought, word, or deed, all this I give away without concern for my own well-being, in order to bring about the liberation of all living beings. *Nirvāṇa* means to give up everything, and my heart yearns for *nirvāṇa*. Since I must give up everything, is it not better to give everything to living beings? —I have dedicated myself to the welfare of all beings. Let them slander me, cast dirt at me, and make me the object of their mockery. Let them kill me if they wish. I have given them my body, so why should I worry about that? Those who scorn me, injure me, or mock at me—may they all achieve enlightenment" (Śāntideva, *Bodhicaryāvatāra*).

The realization of the bodhisattva path entails the overcoming of all narrow individual limitations, as well as the recognition of supraindividual realities (and thus, too, of powers transcending the individual) in our own mind. Thus one attitude is required from the beginning of anyone wishing to tread the bodhisattva path—an attitude that is free from all egocentricity and universally oriented. Anyone who only seeks his own liberation, or who wishes to escape from suffering by the shortest route, without regard for the sufferings of his fellow beings, has by such an attitude already deprived himself of the most essential means toward the achievement of his goal. It is only through turning away from even the subtlest forms of egocentric striving and through the development of the Four Divine Abidings (*brahmavihāras*) that the way becomes open.

It is not a question of debating whether it is really objectively possible to liberate the whole world. Even the Buddha was unable to achieve this during his lifetime. But the universality of his genius had such a lasting effect that his presence can be felt to this day, and the process of liberation he set in motion twenty-five hundred years ago continues and will still continue as long as there are beings who have need of it. In this sphere it is not the achievement that is important, but only the spiritual attitude that is determined by the bodhisattva ideal and that finds expression in the fact that every individual plays his part to the best of his knowledge and ability, without reservation or restriction, toward achieving the supreme goal. Such a person must be constantly aware that each one of his efforts must be aimed at the well-being of all. And even when we have reached the realm of the highest bliss we shall not cease to work for the welfare of all, but shall still share their joys and sorrows and point out the way to liberation for them.

In the Buddhist canonical scriptures it is stated that even the quiet passing away of an *arahat* brings blessings to the world, and that is undoubtedly true. But why did the Buddha return to the world from the Bodhi Tree and take upon himself all the troubles of the life of a wandering ascetic, if the spiritual effect of his enlightenment had alone already exhausted all the possibilities of service he could perform for humanity? Does not this great, supreme sacrifice show that *nirvāṇa* by itself cannot be regarded as the highest ideal of Buddhism?

The more Buddhism developed its own spiritual world by following up the practical, logical and metaphysical consequences of its fundamental principles, the more the idea of *nirvāṇa* receded before the ideal of the bodhisattva. For *nirvāṇa* is—if we go beyond the definition of the extinction of greed, hatred, and delusion—a goal shared by Buddhism with other Indian salvific systems. But the bodhisattva ideal gives Buddhism that characteristic feature that distinguishes it from all other Indian schools, and which carried it victoriously beyond the frontiers of India, so that it became one of the great spiritual and cultural forces of mankind.

The power of the bodhisattva ideal, which conquered the then known Asiatic world in a peaceful campaign of conquest previously unknown, is above all to be sought in the fact that it combines within itself universal love, boundless compassion for all beings, and the quest for enlightenment, thus appealing to the heart and mind of every independently thinking human being. In this context the experiential realm of *nirvāṇa* becomes a component on the way to total enlightenment, and is thus ranged within the universality of the enlightenment experience. For the essence of *samyak-sambodhi* allows of no exclusivity, can be neither gained nor possessed, and radiates boundlessly and inexhaustibly in all directions, thus allowing all others to share in its light and warmth, just as the sun gives out its light and warmth without limit to all who have eyes to see and the capacity to feel its warmth and receive its life-giving power.

Just like the sun, which illuminates our world without making distinctions, yet has a different effect on different beings in accordance with their receptivity and their degree of opening up, so it is with the activity of the enlightened one. Though he embraces all beings in his mind without distinction, nevertheless he knows that not all can be immediately liberated at the same time: the seed of enlightenment that he scatters will bear fruit sooner in one and later in another, in accordance with the receptivity or maturity of the different beings. However, since in the experience of enlightenment time is as illusory as space, the enlightened one preempts the enlightenment of all that lives in the experience of *samyak-sambodhi*. This is the universality of buddhahood and the fulfillment of the bodhisattva vow.

But for one who has, under the profound influence of the *bodhicitta*, taken this vow upon himself in his heart, and declared for the bodhisattva ideal, the figure of the Buddha will henceforth stand in the middle of his religious life. For him this figure will represent the embodiment of the lofty goal whose realization is the task of every disciple of the Exalted One.

The inner content of Buddhism is not seen here in the timeless and spaceless confines of abstract thought, nor as a dogma sanctified by antiquity, but rather in its spatial and temporal breadth, development, and expansion, that is, in the living growth of its thought and feeling and its confrontation with life—in short, in its universality. We are not concerned here with whatever may be urged by philosophical speculation on the question of the reality or unreality of the world, its relation to the spiritual experience, or about the "state" of liberation or of "final *nirvāṇa*." The one and only thing of consequence for the disciple on this path is the fact that what we intuitively seek to grasp under the labels "perfection," "enlightenment," or "buddhahood" actually was once achieved by a human being, and that therefore it must be possible for *any* human being similarly to reach this very same lofty goal.

But, as we have already seen, this path is not one of flight from the world, but a path of overcoming the world through growing understanding and wisdom (*prajñā*), through active charity (*maitrī*), through a profound sharing of the sorrows and joys of others (*karuṇā, muditā*), as well as through equanimity (*upekṣā*) toward one's own weal and woe. The guide and example on this path is the figure of the Buddha. For, however much the dogmatists of the different schools may argue and debate, what greater assurance can we have than in following the example of the Enlightened One? From his exemplary life we increasingly gain the inner certainty that we too are called to, and capable of gaining, the supreme enlightenment, if we tear down the self-created rigid boundaries of our ego and so make ourselves free of all fear. *Fearlessness* is the most prominent characteristic of all bodhisattvas and all who tread the bodhisattva path. For them life has lost its terrors and suffering its sting. Instead of scorning earthly existence, or condemning its "imperfection," they fill it with a new meaning.

They have realized that it is not only conceited but foolish to condemn life as evil and reject it, to deny one's higher capacities for unfoldment, before one has even begun to approach an understanding of the whole, and before one has fully developed the highest capabilities of consciousness and reached that illumination that is the flower, fruit, and fulfillment of all existence. The action of those who strike out in the opposite direction is comparable to that of people who bite into an unripe fruit. They throw it away and declare that all fruits of this kind are uneatable, instead of awaiting the time of ripening.

Another danger should be mentioned. Owing to a wrong interpretation of the *anātman* doctrine, individuality is often regarded, especially by Western Buddhists, as an inhibiting factor on the path of the Dharma, because the development of one's individuality is equated with ego-attachment. Quite apart from the fact that the Buddha was called by his contemporaries *Mahāpuruṣa,* meaning a great personality, individual and unmistakable and towering over others of his time, so too many of his great disciples and followers, who had reached the supraindividual, universal level of enlightenment, were people who had developed their individuality by inner realization. They appear to us as unique embodiments of a creative experience.

On the bodhisattva path one must avoid all extremes and, in conformity with the Teacher's doctrine, follow the Noble Middle Path. Therefore those who repress the activity of the senses and their natural life-functions before making any attempt to use them properly are just as far from reaching the state of sanctity as those who indulge in unrestrained sensuality. While the latter lose themselves in subhuman realms, the former turn into fossils. A sanctity that depends only on negative virtues, merely on avoidance and refraining, may impress the multitude as an example of self-control and strength of mind. It may even lead to complete self-extinction, but not to enlightenment, because it is a way of stagnation and spiritual death. It is liberation from suffering at the cost of life and the living spark of enlightened mind within us.

The becoming aware of this spark of *bodhicitta* is the beginning of the bodhisattva path, which brings about the liberation from suffering and from the fetters of egohood not by a denial of life, but by serving one's neighbor in the course of striving for perfect enlightenment, for when this spark shines forth in the depths of our consciousness, it initiates the process of enlightenment by transforming the latent, potential powers in us into active, all-penetrating energies, as a result of which existence ceases to be a meaningless roundabout. But to enable us to penetrate into that realm of potential powers, the Buddha and his great disciples have shown a way that gives us insights into the depths of our consciousness. In the mediatative process we come to understand that our worldview and world understanding are a product of our consciousness. This reveals to us that the world we live in corresponds to our own mental condition; in other words, we live in a world that we, as it were, create afresh every moment, and have thus "deserved."

The way out of this misery cannot therefore be by trying to escape from this world, but by purifying our consciousness and by a turning about within. This, however, is only possible if we understand the nature of our mind and of the forces that operate in it. We then realize that the mind that is capable of recognizing the light of stars millions of light-years away is no less wonderful than the nature of that light itself. And how much greater still is the miracle of that inner light that slumbers in the depths of our consciousness! To penetrate this depth and to awaken this profound conscious in ourselves—that is the aim of the *bodhisattvamārga*, the path to the realization of awakening, liberation, and enlightenment: the path of the breakthrough to the Buddha nature within ourselves.

If certain circles in Buddhist orthodoxy still maintain to this day that the attainment of perfect enlightenment can only be gained by a single individual in the course of many thousands of years, so that it is quite futile to aim at such a goal, this is nothing but an admission of spiritual poverty and dogmatic rigidity. A religion whose ideal is only a matter of the past or the distant future has no living value for the present day. And so the Dharma, by being separated from the living personality of the Buddha, has been dehumanized and made into a pseudoscientific system of negative values and "special cases." In such a system, meditation can easily turn into a morbid, destructive analysis in which everything living is dissected and fragmented until it is resolved into rotting matter or the functions and complexes of a senseless mechanism.

The person on the bodhisattva path will avoid this danger without falling into the other extreme. In accordance with reality, he will see the impermanence of all compounded things and their conditioned origin, and will not shut his mind to the unpleasant aspects of existence. He will recognize old age, disease, and death as lawful aspects of this existence and not repress these phenomena from his consciousness. For this reason the great masters of the Vajrayāna preferred to use charnel grounds and cremation places for their meditation. They did this not in order to practice disgust, but to get familiar with all aspects of existence, including impermanence as a process that has to be regarded as something natural, without emotionally colored evaluation.

They also sought out these places because other people avoided them from terror or disgust, so that they could practice absorption undisturbed. Further, for their pupils such locations were places for exercises in overcoming revulsion and fear, and for gaining instead equanimity and an unclouded view of reality. The canonical scriptures tell us that even the Buddha, during the time of his mental preparation, deliberately went to such remote and uncanny places in order, as he himself tells us, to overcome fear. Lingering at such places—as well as the meditative observation of corpses in the different stages of putrefaction or other gruesome things—only makes sense if it leads the meditator to such fearlessness as will enable him to face reality as it is and to come to know things in their true nature, without desire or aversion.

But the purpose of such contemplations is ruined if the contemplator cannot rid his mind of disgust, revulsion, and terror. Driving out desire with revulsion is driving out the devil with Beelzebub. There is probably scarcely anyone who feels revulsion at the sight of dead leaves or dried-up flowers. And our joy in blossoms and flowers is not reduced because we know they are impermanent. On the contrary, our knowledge of the perishability of these tender growths makes their blossoming even more precious to us, just as the fleetingness of the moment in human life gives it a particular value. And for this very reason, according to the doctrine of the diamond vehicle, it is the task of man to make our perishable body a place for the imperishable, a temple of the spirit.

This process of transformation takes place in the Vajrayāna by the creation of those peaceful and wrathful images that are known as mahāsattva-bodhisattvas. In the act of identification these figures increasingly become, in the existence of the meditator, a source of mental delight. Through creative concentration the *sādhaka* creates in them a center of spiritual power that extends beyond the particular experience to exert an effect on the outside world, while transforming the meditator.

Since we awaken these great bodhisattva figures to life for ourselves in meditation, we call them dhyāni-bodhisattvas.* Every single one of them, as for example Avalokiteśvara, Mañjuśrī or Maitreya, is the specific embodiment of a particular aspect of the spirit of bodhisattvahood. For, just as human individuals with similar ideals and outlook may have very different characters, so too these bodhisattvas, although they are all embodiments of sympathy, of all-embracing compassion, of active charity and all-seeing and all-penetrating wisdom, nevertheless give expression to

---

**Bodhi* = "enlightenment"; *sattva* = "essence, being"; *dhyāna* = "meditation." Thus the dhyāni-bodhisattvas are "essences of enlightenment produced or seen in meditation," which appear in corporeal form.

these aspects of the enlightened consciousness in uniquely different ways.

They have all perfected the unity of *upāya* and *prajñā* (*upāya* being the all-embracing and compassionate fellow-feeling with all beings [= Mahākaruṇā]), but they differ in the way one or another aspect is emphasized. Common to them all is the knowledge of the essential unity of all life, which grows from the ability to put oneself in the place of another. Whoever has passed through this path of bodhisattvahood by means of developing vision and identification is one who is liberated and released. He is one who has not merely gained "sanctity" or "freedom from the defilements" in the traditional sense, and with it mere deliverance from suffering—he is one who has attained to perfect enlightenment and the realization of universal consciousness. The breakthrough to this liberating awakening presupposes that all individual limitations have been overcome and that the supraindividual realities have been experienced in one's own mind. And since the experience of this awakening is the most universal experience the human mind is capable of, it demands from the very beginning a basic attitude that opens up without limit to life in its universality.

Let us recall once again that the Buddha, in his first sermon in the Deer Park near Vārāṇasi, spoke of *anuttara sammā-sambodhi* (supreme perfect enlightenment), and not of a negative *nirvāṇa* that consisted merely of the cessation of the *āśravas* (worldly influences, human passions) and of suffering. This, whenever it is mentioned here, is referred to as a mere accompaniment of perfect enlightenment.

We must also remember that what the Buddha expressed and could express in words was only a fraction of what he taught through his personality and example. But even the teaching and example together of this great personality reflect merely a fraction of his spiritual experience. The Buddha was well aware of the inadequacy of words when at first he hesitated to proclaim his doctrine and put it into words. For what he had seen was, in his own words, "profound, hard to understand, hard to realize, not to be grasped by the understanding alone." And when he finally decided to teach the truth out of compassion for those few "with little dust on their eyes," he deliberately avoided making statements about the "last things."

He refused to answer questions concerning the supramundane realm of spiritual realization, and was also silent about problems that passed beyond the scope of human understanding. Being no friend of purely speculative thought, he confined himself to pointing out a way that could be trodden, one that provided the possibility of solving all genuine problems. He presented this path in such a way that its understanding was adapted to the intellectual and emotional capacities of his listeners. He guided his pupils according to their individual stage of development, passing on the profounder aspects of the Dharma as well as instructions for higher meditation only to the narrow circle of more advanced pupils.

Later schools of Buddhism remained faithful to this principle. They adapted the teaching methods and meditative exercises to the needs both of the individual and of the mental or historically conditioned development of their time. And just as the Buddha himself had guided his disciples differently according to their spiritual maturity, giving them different practices, so too the later schools kept the more difficult aspects of their teachings and the corresponding meditation practices for those who had developed the necessary knowledge and skills.

These advanced teachings were then labeled as esoteric or "secret" doctrines. But there was no intention, with this practice, of preventing anyone from gaining higher stages of realization. Rather, this method was based on the desire to avoid idle chatter and mere speculation by which the untrained might easily be misled into intellectually anticipating higher states of consciousness without going to the trouble of acquiring them through their own meditative practice. For the intellectual anticipation of unrealized mental spiritual experiences can easily lead the inexperienced to suppose that they have, through conceptual understanding, already done what was necessary, and this blocks the process of meditative experience which alone releases the energy necessary for transformation.

Whoever today wishes to follow the bodhisattva path must learn, following in the Buddha's footsteps, to keep his mind continually open by the practice of constant mindfulness. He must train himself, through study (*vitarka-vicāra*, *dharmavicaya*, *viveka*, the gaining of *jñāna* and *vidyā*), through moral conduct based on personal responsibility (*śīla*, *pāramitās*, *brahmavihāras*), through cultic devotion and ritual (*pūjā*), and through meditation (*śamatha*, *vipaśyanā*, *smṛti*, *bhāvanā*, *dhyāna*, *samādhi*), to avoid any one-sidedness, and to strive hard for inner unification and transformation in order so to gain a worldview wide enough to embrace the totality of human knowledge. On this way of increasing spiritual profundity he will be able to penetrate to the heart of all appearances, while his way of life will enable him to make use of every activity of body and mind as a help on the path to enlightenment.

On the preparatory stages of the path, which activate both the intellectual and the emotional powers of man, he will learn to use clear thinking as a regulative element for the mind, and as a sure foundation on which intuitive experience can unfold. He will utilize his emotional nature as the motive power of his activity in the form of complete devotion to the goal. He will master his thought by learning to master its laws, in order then to pass beyond the bounds of all thinking and speculation and to devote himself to a clear and wide-awake consciousness of suffering beings. Then, one day, the *bodhicitta* may spontaneously arise in him. This suddenly bursts forth in a person who is sufficiently open, in the form of a complete and "total" state of being wholly possessed by the pain and suffering of all beings. Then all personal troubles, all torments and pain seem unimportant. His consciousness is filled with only one wish: to make all these beings free and happy.

The experience of being thus wholly possessed, which leaves room for nothing else, has a profound effect on the person experiencing it. Even when the experience has long since passed like the sound of a bell that struck only once, and when the world has again long since demanded its tribute, it still remains the determining and directing force in the life of the person to whom it has happened.

But we do not usually come to this experience that breaks our ego apart through rules or vows—not even by taking upon oneself eighteen fundamental and forty-four subsidiary vows. Formulas, fixations, vows, and rules are always the product of ages of decline in which the immediate experience has vanished and people have tried to capture in the net of forms and ceremonies what has long since eluded them. And so, with every formula, we only erect even thicker walls around the self-created prison that we have made out of the desire for security, and which finally leaves no room to maneuver.

If there is anything in this world that can prepare the way for the *bodhicitta*, it is nothing but a loving, understanding opening up to and empathy with all beings, which does not take possession of them or seek any reward for itself, however subtle, and certainly does not think of "gaining merit." Egoless action with clear consciousness, out of love, compassion, and shared joy with all sentient beings—this is the only key. And whoever succeeds in loving even a single being selflessly without making demands or seeking selfish ends—such a person becomes capable through this love for one being to love all beings, and so to produce the *bodhicitta*, or rather, to let it break through. And then he will perhaps find similar words to those once uttered by Śāntideva:

> I take upon myself the burden of all suffering.
> I am determined to bear it.
> I shall not turn back.
> I shall not flee or tremble.
> I shall not yield or hesitate.
> Why? Because the liberation of all beings is my vow.

5 | *The Meaning of Ritual, Liturgy, and Initiation in Buddhism*

The Buddha repeatedly drew attention to the dangers of "clinging to moral rules and rituals" (Pali *sīlabbata-parāmāsa*). He regarded the belief that one could gain enlightenment and liberation merely through moral behavior and the performance of rituals as one of the four attachments (*upādāna*),* which merely make a person's liberation more difficult. He also included this "clinging to (moral) rules and rituals" among the ten fetters (Pali *saṃyojana*)† by which the worldling (*puthujjana*) is bound to the world of *saṃsāra*. In fact, he further stressed the importance of not "clinging to rules and rituals" by stating that it was only by the overcoming of this fetter, together with the abandonment of the false belief in an eternal, unchanging soul or personality (Pali *sakkāya-diṭṭhi*) and of doubt (Pali *vicikicchā*) that "stream-entry" (Pali *sotāpatti*)‡ could be gained, through which anyone (monk, nun, *upāsaka*) is changed from a worldling to a "noble disciple" (*ariya-puggala*).

This statement of the Buddha's, however, does not mean that morality and all kinds of ritual are in themselves an obstacle on the path to liberation; it merely points out that morality and ritualism can only be wholesome when, supported by a full

---

*The four attachments: sensual attachment, attachment to views, attachment to rules and rituals, attachment to the belief in an eternal ego.

†The ten fetters that bind beings to the cycle of rebirths are (1) ego-belief of two kinds: (a) "eternity-belief" (*sassata-diṭṭhi,* belief in an eternal unchanging ego) and (b) "annihilation-belief" (*uccheda-diṭṭhi,* the belief in a self that depends on the five groups of existence [*khandhas*] and is therefore annihilated at their dissolution), (2), doubt, (3) attachment to (moral) rules and rituals, (4), sensuality, (5) ill-will, (6) desire for the fine-material sphere (*rūparāga*), (7) desire for the immaterial sphere (*arūparāga*), (8) conceit and pride, (9) inner agitation, (10) ignorance.

‡The state of a *sotāpanna*. "One who is on the way to abandoning the first three fetters and thus to attain stream-entry, or one who has overcome these three fetters—such a person is called *sotāpanna*" (*Puggala Paññatti* 1.47).

realization of the nature of reality, they are consciously employed as a means on the path to enlightenment. But if a person becomes attached to such means in the belief that they were themselves a certain path to liberation, he would become dependent on them and his ego would become inflated, a condition from which it is difficult to get free. The same applies to a person who follows moral rules and rituals simply out of habit, tradition, or routine, or even to satisfy an aesthetic urge.

If we want to understand this question of "not clinging to moral rules and rituals" aright, we must put the accent not on "rules and rituals" (Pali *sīlabbata*) but on "attachment" (*parāmāsa*) or "clinging" (*upādāna*). Ritual cultic actions have been a part of the community life since the earliest days of Buddhism. Thus, for example, the triple refuge in Buddha, Dharma, and Sangha was regarded from the very beginning as something so important that every Buddhist performed this ritual, and does so to this day.

In the Bhikkhu Sangha too, rituals were always considered important. Thus the *upasampadā*, by means of which the novice (Pali *sāmaṇera*) was elevated to the status of a fully-ordained *bhikkhu*, was for centuries kept secret, and no monk not fully ordained was allowed to be present at this ceremony. This ritual was regularly held on a specially consecrated platform away from the area accessible to the public.

Other rituals, too, were highly regarded from the earliest times of Buddhism, and there were special ceremonies such as *pūjā* and *paritta*—the latter being for the protection of body and mind. In a similar way we find early references to the ritual of circumambulating religious buildings (Skt. *pradakṣina*), along with the veneration of symbols of the Buddha with candles, flowers, and incense, as well as bowing before them and the ritual recitation of religious texts that is familiar to every Buddhist.

The practice of these rituals with perfect, heartfelt devotion was always regarded—as was living in the spirit of the *śīlas*—as a "wholesome" way of action on the noble path of the Buddha. But the Buddha was well aware of the weaknesses of human nature and the self-made nets in which human beings are continually being trapped. And so he made it clear that even what was "wholesome," when wrongly used, could work against one, so that what normally appears as a means of liberation can become a subtle but hard-to-break fetter. For we might imagine that by strictly observing the rules of morality or the practice of certain rituals we had gained some special merits and had thus become better people or even saints, or that we had magically influenced the laws of the world. Anyone who thinks thus and acts accordingly has turned what was wholesome into a poison: he has erected his ego even higher and strengthened its position in the face of the world, instead of weakening such structures and rendering them transparent.

The Buddha's warning not to become attached to rules and rituals was nowhere taken more seriously than in the Chinese Ch'an school (from which the Japanese Zen school arose), and in the *siddha* movement that developed out of the Vajrayāna, which in turn influenced the later Vajrayāna itself in this direction. The preserved biographies of the *siddhas* and of the great Vajrayānis such as Tilopa, Naropa, Marpa, and Milarepa make this just as clear as do the legendary tales of the old Ch'an and Zen masters.

And yet, in both Zen and Vajrayāna, rites and rules play a large part and great emphasis is laid on their observance. Thus the Zen monk, after a course of study, is instructed to leave aside all canonical writings and all learning, in order to develop without prejudice to these a spiritual honesty and spontaneity. And all this is taught to him in a style of expression whose exaggerations and paradoxical formulations come as a shock. Yet on the other hand the daily round of the Zen monk is dictated by minutely fixed rules and rites that accompany him from arising in the morning to going to bed at night and never let him go: there is the ritual of eating, of cleaning the eating bowls, of entering the Zen hall, of sitting down, of sitting, of *sūtra* recitation, the repeated recitation of the vows, the prostrations before images of the Buddha and of Mañjuśrī as well as the ritual veneration of the master and the forms of mutual greeting. In other words, even the school that is supposed to lay least store by rituals in fact insists on the strictest forms of religious ritual and insists on a life for its followers that is dominated by rules and rituals. Western admirers and followers of the seemingly so unorthodox ways of Zen ought to spend just a short period in a Zen monastery in order to be cured of their misapprehensions.

The ceremonial ritualism which Zen has developed to aesthetic perfection is found even more in Vajrayāna, although in a way that emphasizes its symbolism more strongly, and that may often give the effect of routine. In view of these facts we must ask ourselves whether such forms are at all compatible with the Buddhist lifestyle as taught by the Founder, and whether we in the West, if we want to make a new beginning here, would not do better to drop them.

Man is a being who, among other things, is the product of historical developments and connections without which he would not be what he is. And precisely in this historical context it has been proved over and over again that rules and rituals can be productive of wholesome forces both for the cultural development of humanity and for the spiritual development of the individual. Thus we continually find afresh that the practice of the five *śīlas* gives our lives a harmony both within and without, provided we follow them consciously in our lives in accordance with our degree of maturity and insight. But we should remain quite clear that these *śīlas* should never be degraded to the level of "commandments" that have to be rigorously obeyed in all circumstances, regardless of the situation. Otherwise we would come to resemble that monk who, strictly following the rule that he must not touch a woman, allowed his mother to drown in a well into which she had fallen while he stood by without stirring a finger.

Only when we understand the reasons for this or that rule, and only when we completely agree with it, should we accept it and act accordingly. The Buddha never expected his disciples to follow him blindly. He was the only founder of a religion who not only allowed criticism but encouraged it in his pupils. He only wanted people to follow him if they did so on the basis of their own experience and conviction.

And so he said to his favorite disciple, Ānanda, "If you were to follow the Dharma purely out of love for me or because you respect me, I would not accept you as a disciple. But if you follow the Dharma because you have yourself experienced its truth, because you understand and act accordingly—only under these conditions have you the right to call yourself a disciple of the Exalted One."

Therefore, in the Buddhist view, moral rules and rituals are wholesome only if they are performed in the right spirit, that is to say with full understanding, with mature insight and clear awareness. For if a ritual is performed simply as a routine or because it is prescribed by tradition or convention, then—since it has lost all meaning—it becomes a meaningless act and therefore a hindrance on the path of real progress. But if a ritual is performed consciously, with perfect understanding of its meaning, then it becomes an act of meditation that is directed outward and is transformed into a course of action on which all the practicer's senses are concentrated.

But if in the course of such a ritual we offer a candle to the Buddha, we should not think or suppose we are doing the Buddha a favor. We should rather be fully aware that we must hold aloft the light we have received from him, which illumines our darkness, so that we and all beings, illumined by that light, may find our way to the goal. In this way the candle offered to the Buddha is, for the person performing the ritual, a means of recalling and being mindful (*smṛti*) of the light of enlightenment that has shone within every one of us without any recognizable beginning, even though darkened by the self-built walls of the ego, which it is necessary to tear down.

The same applies, *mutatis mutandis*, to the presentation of incense and other offerings, through which we declare our thankfulness, our devotion, and our readiness to follow self-sacrificingly in the footsteps of the Enlightened One, in order to allow the slumbering capacities for buddhahood to break through in us. And when we look at the image of the Buddha, we should regard it as something to remind us of the potential buddhahood within ourselves, of the great ideal that the historical buddha Śākyamuni realized in his own life, and to the realization of which we too are called in our lives. For the goal of enlightenment is within the reach of every conscious being. But it would be foolish to suppose that by venerating his image we are performing a service to the Buddha. Rather, by such veneration we strengthen our own purpose to follow in his path and realize the Dharma, which is not simply his teaching, but is also the universal law of macrocosm and microcosm as this appears to us on the human plane.

The Buddhist Dharma is based on the knowledge of the "nonsubstantiality" of all phenomena. As long as we regard matter and mind as irreconcilable opposites, we split the world into two halves and lose the ground from under our feet. Thus shaping and giving form is the basis of all experiencing and knowing. Ritual is just one of the ways of giving form, through which we give expression to our deepest thoughts and feelings, and so it must be the product either of clear thought or of genuine, spontaneous feeling. Otherwise rituals become empty repetitions of conventional forms accompanied by what is for the practicer an empty babble of words, while his thoughts are elsewhere, and in this way the whole thing becomes an obstacle on the path to enlightenment.

Only if we are able to see every word, every gesture, every observed form, and every ritual object as a symbol that increasingly leads us to further insight into our innermost nature and thus, making us more mature through the experience, transforms us—only so does the ritual become a valuable instrument on our way. It strengthens our power of concentration, enables us to gain intuitive insight, and through imagery leads us to that freedom of all images that, symbolically, we call *mahāmudrā*, "the great gesture." In this way, *mantras*, *mudrās*, and *maṇḍalas* become aids (*upāya*) just as meaningful as the *mani-khorlo* (the so-called "prayer wheel"), the beads of a rosary, or the altar on which we perform our *pūjā*, or as the psychocosmic ritual structure of a *stūpa* that we circumambulate in the direction of the sun.

These aids and symbols, when they are incorporated in a ritual that has developed in a living tradition and is consciously practiced, can be of great assistance for one treading that path. But only when the ritual is celebrated with *devotion* can it bring immediate intuitive understandings that, by transforming body and mind, lead to a stage of development that can no longer be expressed in words.

The performance of a *pūjā* ritual takes place in Buddhism on several levels simultaneously. In the first place, it is an expression of reverence and gratitude to the great trailblazers of the spirit, the buddhas and bodhisattvas, and all who trod the holy path for the welfare of all beings. From this reverence and gratitude the wish arises to tread this path oneself and to realize it. So the second step on this path is the dedication of one's own person, the vow to devote oneself to the service of the enlightened ones, their teaching and their community. The necessary goal-oriented work on ourselves leads us into meditation. And here we come to know the third and most important aspect of a *pūjā*: the possibility of experiencing the ritual as a visible representation, a "dramatized" meditation, in which the cultic action becomes a means to concentration, as a way of proceeding further along the holy path.

Through the parallelism of bodily, psychic, and spiritual actions by means of words, gestures, thoughts, and feelings, a singleness of direction of consciousness is attained, which affects not only our superficial consciousness (the intellect and the knowledge and contents of consciousness brought in by the senses), but also the deeper levels of our psyche. With regular practice of such a ritual, our whole being becomes slowly and steadily transformed, and made receptive to the powers of the light of enlightenment (*bodhicitta*). And so *pūjā* (as all Buddhist schools are agreed) is one possible way into meditation, which—because it draws in the whole person and points that person toward the goal—is not exhausted in the remembering and becoming conscious of what the Buddha showed us by his example, nor is it merely a renewal of our vow to tread this path with all our might; it is in addition a further step toward the realization of inner unity and integration.

In order to gain the full benefit of this possibility, we must continually rethink and reexperience the *pūjā*. In this process the multifariousness and indeed the inexhaustibility of its symbolism must be repeatedly experienced in all its facets, and in this way the ritual will become a source of ever new intuitions. But the *pūjā* can only perform this task if we always carry it out with a "beginner's mind" without becoming fixated on recognitions and insights we have once gained, or without expecting similar experiences as before. For then we would block the free flow of creative experience and the—in itself—inexhaustible source of inner creation, whose free flowing forth alone can feed the process of continual change, integration, illumination, and transparency.

In performing *pūjā*, a Buddhist is clear that he is not "making magic." He knows quite clearly that mantric formulas, *mudrās*, and symbolic acts such as the lighting of candles, the "transformation" of water into *amṛta* (the water of immortality), or the presentation of incense, flowers, and offerings are effective only by way of one's own mind: through the harmonious cooperation of form (including also sound and rhythm), feeling (impulse and religious devotion), and idea (mental associations derived from knowledge and experience), whereby the latent psychic powers (of which those subject to the conscious will form the smallest part) are awakened, strengthened, and transformed.

Form is here essential because it is the vessel that contains the other qualities. Feeling is essential because it creates a unity, just as the heat of fire melts the most various metals and combines them in a new, homogeneous unity. The idea, on the other hand, is the "substance," the *prima materia* that gives life to all elements of the human mind and awakens their sleeping powers. If we use the word "idea" here, this should not be understood in the sense of a mental abstraction, but in the original sense of the Greek word *eidos*, as a creative image, or as a form of living experience in which reality is mirrored and continually created afresh.

Whereas the form of a liturgy or a ritual has become crystallized from the practice of many generations, and has been involved in the course of thousands of years in a continual process of change, the *idea* that stands behind the changing forms and continually inspires them afresh is the gift of the Buddha. But the fire that is set ablaze, through the creative qualities of mind and heart and those creative powers that grow from the Buddha's gift, is the part that the pupil has to contribute. Only if his faith, born of inner certainty, and his confidence in the doctrine are pure will he succeed in creating the inner unity. But if his mind is untrained, he will remain incapable of receiving and developing the idea. If he is spiritually obtuse, the inner powers will not respond to the call. And if he lacks concentration he will not be able to harmonize heart, mind, and form.

Thus, the Buddhist ritual in all its parts is not a method of avoiding unpleasant effects of life or dodging the consequences of our actions, but a means of assistance on our path which demands consistent effort and struggle. Only when its essence is clearly perceived in the consciousness of the practicer can the ritual, either as a whole or in any of its parts—*mantras*, *mudrās*, *maṇḍalas*, and all the ritual symbols and actions—be of any use. Anyone who tries to misuse the *pūjā* or any parts of it for selfish ends creates negative forces that will fall back on him. Thus, karma and the negative consequences of an action cannot be removed by mumbling *mantras* or by the use of any kind of religious ritual or magical powers. It is only through purity of heart and sincere spiritual striving that the path of liberation and enlightenment can be perfected. We are warned by the words of Milarepa:

> What's the use of religious rites
> if body, speech, and mind do not accord with Dharma?
> What good can religious rites do
> if anger is not overcome by its opposite?
> What is the use of crying out, "Oh Compassion!"
> if we don't love others more than our own self?

There are teachers today in the East and the West who give their pupils mantras without initiating them into their direction and meaning. Such meaningless repetition of a symbolic sound leads at best to a hypnoid state of relaxation. *Mantras*, *mudrās*, and *maṇḍalas* are aids to meditation. If they are turned into objects of blind faith or into means of achieving worldly gain, they have lost their true meaning. The Buddha placed the human being in the center of his world system—a human being who can gain liberation only by his own efforts and not by divine intervention or magic. If the ritual or any of its parts is misused in this way, it misses the meaning and spirit of the Buddha's teaching and becomes a fetter instead of a possible means of liberation.

But it was precisely this reproach, that the rituals had a "magical" character, that the Indological and Tibetological research of the West raised against the liturgies of the Vajrayāna of both Tibet and Japan. They were interpreted partly as theurgic and demonological invocations, and certain parts of the *pūjā* were compared with the transubstantiation of the Christian Eucharist.

It is true that the Tantras really do speak of the figures produced and seen in meditation as *devas,* that is, "divine presences" or "gods." But the term *deva* has nothing to do with the God-concept of the Near Eastern monotheistic religions. *Devas* are, for people belonging to the Indian cultural sphere, beings who, like all other beings, are caught up in the cycle of rebirths. According to the Tantric teaching, they are brought to life when we call upon them, give them form in our consciousness, and venerate them, even if they have never existed before, and they will die when they are no longer called upon, even if they have lived on for thousands of years in human consciousness. For invoking and venerating them as a means of developing one's visionary powers are acts of mental creation through concentration on an idea, an image, a symbol, or even an emotion.

This visualization has the greatest transforming power when all these elements come together integrated, and it is ineffective if the invocation sinks to a mere mechanical act or intellectual playacting. But the meditatively correct ritual is a means of creating a form through which idea, image, symbol, and emotion are united, integrated, and activated. And so the ritual can become a key that gives us the power and the potentiality of those divine beings produced through meditation. And this is the reason why in previous centuries people who still had some understanding of the processes in the mental sphere kept such rituals secret, for the protection of the uninitiated, and only passed them on to qualified pupils.

Genuine rituals are not "made up"—they grow out of the spontaneous experience of certain highly developed individuals.

In the course of time they accumulate the experiences and practice of generations, and continually expand. But in general they crystallize around the simple core of a symbol or of a simple symbolic action, which was the spontaneous response to a profound feeling or a transforming awareness. This core is often, in periods of decline, buried under a mass of inessentials, and this marks the death of the ritual.

In the Tantra the most important rituals are those that call forth a mental image. They possess creative power, because they affect both the conscious and the unconscious human abilities. This effect is both individual and collective, subjective and objective. Having said this, we have now touched on the question of what "reality" actually is. From the basic point of view of Tantra it really does not matter whether the gods exist outside of our consciousness or not. Even the question of whether we can intellectually prove the existence of these gods or not is of no consequence. For here, in the realm of the psychic, only that is "real" or "actual" that *acts* by way of creation or as a power. From this point of view, an image, a symbol, or a ritual that takes hold of thousands of minds and is capable of transforming people must be regarded as "active reality."

The higher powers invoked through a ritual, which appear to consciousness in the form of visions, are archetypes that through thousands of years of veneration have taken firm root in the collective, supraindividual consciousness, and now lie in readiness to be set free by invocation, so that their inherent, transforming energy can become effective. Thus, invocation has in Buddhism the same function as prayer in the theistic religions. And just as prayer is a communication, a conversation with God, so the Buddhist invocation is a calling on the inner powers from an intense desire for the highest state of perfection—perfect enlightenment. It gains its strength from the polar tension that arises from the awareness of our inadequacy and imperfection on the one hand and our ideal of perfection and wholeness on the other. Thus it is the first goal-directed approach to the immeasurable store of experience of the universal depth-consciousness.

But the ritual does not exert its transforming power on the practicer by the word alone. It takes total possession of him, and must take total possession of him, if it is to develop its full power. Through the coordination of gesture, word, and thought, through the cooperation of body, speech, and mind as well as through the harmony of feeling, verbal expression, and creative imagination in the development of the vision, we achieve the integration of all the functions of our conscious existence. Through this, not only the surface of our personality is approached, but also the deeper strata of our consciousness, so that through the regular practice of the ritual our whole being undergoes a gradual transformation, which leads us step by step to deeper levels of absorption until the final, imageless vision is realized.

From earliest times a key position among the rituals was occupied by the rituals of initiation. From the first days of humanity, these power-giving, impulsive, and transforming rites gave the approach to higher levels of learning and experiencing. They raised the adolescent to the status of a recognized, equal member of the tribe or clan, they informed the future priest, tribal chief, or king with the *mana* or charisma of his office and provided the neophyte in the mystery fellowships with protection and power, so that he was able to confront all the dangers of the inner path.

In Buddhism, too, such initiation rituals have obviously played a part from the very beginning. Thus in the *Dīgha Nikāya* 16.5.30 we read how a wandering ascetic said to Ānanda, "It is a great gain for you all, it is very profitable for you all, that you have obtained the consecration of discipleship in the Teacher's presence." This "consecration" or "sprinkling" (Skt. *abhiṣeka*) was in Vedic times employed, for example, at the consecration of a king, whose head was wetted with holy water, in order thus to convey to him the power and charisma of royalty.

And quite early on, the Buddha spoke of his disciples as sons and daughters of the *ārya-kula*, the noble family of those who were called to spiritual lordship. Those who were "born from his mouth" entered on the heritage of their spiritual father. And so, in the course of the further development of Buddhism in India, disciples were called to be followers of the Buddha through *abhiṣeka*, and thus received the strength to prepare for their coming task: to become a Buddha for the good of the world, a world ruler *(cakravartin)* in the inner realm.

Especially through the development of the Vajrayāna the *abhiṣeka* became a source of strength that opened the door to a long process of spiritual training. Through it the essential experiences and the concentrated knowledge of generations of spiritual teachers are passed on as an inspiring impulse, especially in the form of the transference of that consciousness that the guru has developed within himself from the impulses of his teachers, and that he now passes on to his pupil by the "transfer of spiritual power" (Tib. *dBang-bskur*); the pupil receives this impulse himself, and then employs it to the extent that he is able to open up to it. But the impulse received gives direction to his efforts and fills him with the necessary enthusiasm to continue striving undistractedly for the lofty goal.

He receives a foretaste of this goal when, in the moment of initiation, he shares in the consciousness and the level of realization of his guru. It is this experience that gives the chela the assurance that the goal is attainable and is worth all the effort. From now on he is no longer a blind seeker, but one who knows where his path is leading him. He is filled with unshakeable confidence (Skt. *śrāddhā*), so that his religious practice *(sādhana)* fills him with profound inner joy and happiness. Now it neither takes on the character of a painful fulfilling of one's duty nor does it degenerate into a routine performance of prescribed religious exercises or recitations of texts.

Therefore the initiation by a real guru lies beyond all differences of schools, sects, and scholastic speculations. It is an awakening to our own inner reality, which—however fleetingly glimpsed—determines the course of our further development and our entire way of life, without the compulsion of external rules. Initiation is therefore the greatest gift a guru has to give, a gift that is far more valuable than any formal ordination on joining a monastic order or any other religious organization. Ordinations can always take place without any *spiritual* qualifications being demanded of either the ordainer or the candidate, provided the candidate is willing to obey the prescribed rules and is not precluded by any kind of physical, moral, or spiritual defects.

The *abhiṣeka*, on the other hand, is a procedure by means of which a new dimension of consciousness opens up before the initiate, which, through the simultaneously communicated information and *mantras*, starts up and keeps in being a dynamic process of transformation. In this connection, *mantras* are (apart from their special character as archetypical symbols of a particular attitude of mind) the crystallized forms of a meditative practice and experience going back hundreds of years. In addition, they receive a special emotional and individual stamp that links guru and chela together. These *mantras*, which accompany the meditation, recall the moment of initiation in the mind of the initiate, and fill him again and again with the power to continue on the path he has set out on.

The "power" that is conveyed by the *abhiṣeka* is only effective in the inner realm, and cannot be misused for personal ends. It is an energy that starts off the transformation process in a person, when that person allows it to take effect within him by opening up to it; such a person then becomes an exponent of supraindividual realization, which can then have an effect on others. For this reason a guru can perform initiations and transfers of power or empowerments only to the extent that he himself has developed these powers in himself by years of strict practice. And a chela can only mature into a guru to the extent that he opens himself up without reservations to the specific inner direction of his guru, and from the electoral affinity of spiritual "sonship" or "daughtership" joins the ranks of those who have entered into the spiritual heritage of the guru.

6 | *Guru and Chela*

According to normal Indian usage, a guru is a man who, after many years of devoted study under a master, has developed his knowledge and skill to such a degree that his personality has matured to a perfection that determines all his activities and enables him to pass on to those who become his pupils or chelas the treasures of the knowledge he has gained in following his teacher.

Based on this definition, it seems at first sight justified to translate the word *guru* (Tib. *blama* pronounced *lama*) as "teacher." But this concept, which stems from our Western civilization, is not a real equivalent. In terms of ancient Indian culture, a guru is more than a teacher in the modern sense of that word. He is not concerned with the mere purveying of profane or intellectual knowledge, the passing on of knowledge that can be learned, but above all with awakening a desire for ever higher understanding and profounder experiencing, whereby phenomena are made manifest in their interrelation, in their mutual conditioning, and in their continually growing, ever renewed integration. Seen in this light, a guru is one who has become one with his knowledge, one who is inspired and inspiring, who himself is the embodiment of what he wishes to convey and pass on. His personality alone suffices to convince us of the high order and value of the ideals he represents, as well as of the possibility of putting them into practice here and now. Whoever approaches him with an open, unprejudiced mind feels that here is a man who gives himself without reserve, whose thinking, speech, and actions form a harmonic unity, and whose self-devotion convinces us in our deepest consciousness of the greatness and holiness of this person who has become one with his knowledge.

Knowledge (Skt. *vidyā*) was regarded in India from the earliest times as something sacred—indeed, divine—that was all-embracing. Thus science and the arts included all areas of life, as for instance the sacred scriptures and their commentaries, ritualism, architecture, eroticism, dance, music, mathematics, astronomy, diplomacy, and yoga. But every branch of the sacred sciences pointed to the whole, to the root that it was man's task to reach. The guru, whatever the field in which he had attained mastery, was accordingly a man who had penetrated to the root, and was thus in a position to bring the essential in phenomena in to the region of his chela's potential experience.

The guru was compared to a tree that, without making any distinctions, readily allowed all to harvest its fruits without expecting anything in return. He is simply there, he offers what he has without pressing it on anybody. The flower does not go to the bees, the bees come to the flower, attracted by the perfume of the blossoms and the smell of the nectar. Likewise, a genuine guru does not go out of his way to seek chelas. They have to come of their own accord and acquire their knowledge, attracted by the perfume of the humanity, wisdom, and love of the master.

Such guruship as this cannot be gained like an academic degree or the mastery of a craft. Industry, persistence, and intelligence are not sufficient here. And so the "empowerment" to teach in the tradition comes only at the end of a long process of development, which regularly begins with the chela, because of an inner affinity, finding himself able to identify with the guru, and therefore to open up in complete trust. If he succeeds in developing the power of self-dedication as did Tilopa, Naropa, Marpa, and Milarepa, the great exemplary figures on the Vajrayāna path, then he will quite naturally mature as a follower in the line of his guru. But if anyone attempts to become a guru out of ambition, he is very far indeed from his goal: the only thing that lies within the range of our will is to strive to become an ever more perfect chela.

In ancient India and the countries of the Indian cultural sphere, chelaship began very early—usually at the age of eight. After consecration as a pupil (Skt. *upanayana*) the pupil entered the household *(āśrama)* of his guru and lived in his house, where he paid for his lessons by doing whatever jobs needed to be done as an unpaid servant. He remained for twelve or more years in this community, and modeled himself on the guru and his wife. Possible developmental faults could be early corrected individually, as the group of chelas was always small and so easily watched over. Thus the process of maturation of the individual could be assisted in accordance with his degree of inner realization at any given moment, without demanding either too much or too little from him. The necessary conveying of information—as in dancing, languages, or mathematics—was incorporated in the general education, whose goal was real "cultivation" ["*Bildung*"], that is, the formation of a socially integrated, fully developing human individuality. Thus the training in this guru-chela relationship aimed at the condition of a free human being with a feeling of communal responsibility, who would serve the whole from the resources of his freedom. We have no schools today that follow this principle. The individual cannot develop in the framework of collectivism, but only in the freedom of a self-responsible, creative human being, one freely joined to the community, who is learning to set free all his potential powers for the service of all beings, in order then to help others to develop similarly. In this way there developed in the *āśramas* of ancient India people who, after years of hard work and purification of character, were finally one day able to continue the work of their guru and to gather disciples around themselves. It is against this historical background that the guru-chela relation must be seen and understood.

In Buddhism, too, the guru-chela relation took a principal place from the beginning, and in the monastic *sangha* it was taken for granted. However, after the passing of the Buddha the relation of the guru—who regularly belonged to the monastic order—to his disciples in household life was often a very loose one. This only changed radically with the rise of the Mahāyāna and the Vajrayāna. But the old *āśrama* system was largely abandoned. The external community was now sublimated to a spiritual family based on the principle of elective affinity. Already the Buddha had called his community of disciples his *ārya-kula*, his "noble family," for anyone who became a chela of the Buddha gave up the caste and family he or she had been born into and became a "son" or "daughter" of the Exalted One. This factor of "rebirth" or "new birth" into the "noble family" was stressed and developed even more strongly with the rise of the Vajrayāna. The guru, who in the Vajrayāna was often not a monk, here took a key position because it was he who made the higher path accessible to the seeker and in this way, as a guide, occupied the position of the Tathāgata. Bhagavatī Lakṣmīṃkarā, Indrabhūti's famous sister and Padmasambhava's aunt, stressed in her work *Advayasiddhi* that the choice of a guru was the most important thing in the life of a spiritual seeker. Neither in the moving nor in the motionless world was there anything more precious than a guru, through whose loving care a wise person could attain to all kinds of perfection.

The relation between guru and chela is like an intact father-son or father-daughter relation, or, since in the Vajrayāna tradition there are also female gurus, like the corresponding relation between a mother and her son or daughter. The basis of such a guru-chela relationship is always an inner meeting, based on spiritual affinity, between two people, which far transcends all family bonds and lasts for a lifetime. It can be neither "cancelled" nor "annulled," because it is not a matter of a "teacher's relation" or a "training agreement," but an inner link that—independent of one's will—can no more be broken off than the blood relationship between father and son, which persists even if the son has long since gone his own way.

Accordingly, entering such a guru-chela relationship is neither a matter of the intellect nor a hasty emotional reaction. Only when both guru and chela intuitively feel in advance the inner bond of feeling and thinking, will any fruitful work be possible. Therefore, the choice of a guru and the acceptance of a chela is something that calls for a high degree of responsibility on both sides, and which can only become fully effective if it is sparked by the flashing forth of that all-maturing cosmogonic eros that introduces and continually supports the process of spiritual transformation.

In Buddhism, and especially in the Mahāyāna and Vajrayāna, a distinction was always made between the instructing teacher who taught beginners the basics of Dharma, the *kalyāṇamitra*, the good friend and guide who helpfully guided the pupil's first faltering steps on the path of Mahāyāna, and the guru as the guide on the higher path of Vajrayāna, whose profoundest teachings are found not in his words, but in what remains unspoken because it transcends speech, yet can be directly experienced in his presence. For, on the basis of his own realization, he has the capacity to activate the latent powers in his pupil and thereby lead him toward enlightenment. He thus becomes an inspirer in the fullest sense of the word, from whose living spirit we catch fire, and who lets us share in his vision of reality.

But in order to convey to his pupils what he himself has experienced and realized, and in order to transmit his own experience, he must be able to renew or recreate it each time he performs the initiation rite (Skt. *abhiṣeka*, Tib. *dBang-bskur*). This requires an extensive preparation—not just an intellectual one, like that of a school or university teacher, who prepares himself by assembling all relevant data on his subject and by mapping out a logical way of presenting those data in the most convincing way. The preparation of a religious teacher consists in putting himself in touch with the deepest sources of spiritual power through intense meditation, during which he *becomes* the embodiment of the force or quality that he wants to transmit.* Such a preparation may take days or weeks, according to the nature of the forces that have to be awakened and made alive in the consciousness of the chela.

Just as the word *guru* means more than "teacher," so, too, a chela is more than a pupil in the ordinary sense. *Chela* (*cela* from Skt. *ceḍa, ceṭa,* "servant") is perhaps better rendered "disciple," in order to bring out the fact that he is linked with his guru by a profound psychic relationship, a link that is further deepened by the initiation rite. For in the initiation a direct transfer of spiritual power takes place, which is regularly embodied in the sacred formula of a *mantra* that is conveyed to the pupil during the initiation. By means of this *mantra* he is able at any time to summon up in himself the transmitted power, so that a permanent contact is maintained with the guru.

However, this psychic power is not some force that overwhelms the consciousness of the chela. It represents the ability of the guru to enable the chela—whose being is spiritually akin to him and therefore, as it were, on the same "wavelength"—to share in his own experience, which belongs to a higher level of consciousness and realization. In this way the chela receives by way of foretaste a lightning glimpse into the nature of the goal that is to be attained, so that he no longer pursues a vague ideal, but works toward a reality that has been perceived and experienced. Such a capacity for transmission, however, can only be developed by means of a life of meditation, and is strengthened by every period of temporary seclusion and spiritual concentration, just like the stored-up energy of the water in a dammed river.

Just as Śakyamuni Buddha, as the first teacher of our world epoch, holds a central place in the thought and feelings of every Buddhist, so, too, that guru who brought about the first, decisive change in his life is always the central figure in the heart of the chela. He is the root guru (Skt. *mūlaguru,* Tib. *tsawai-bLama*),

---

*See *The Way of the White Clouds* (Shambhala, 1970), pp. 157–158.

with whom the chela, on the basis of inner kinship, can largely identify so that, following his inner development, he enters into the succession of that guru and, provided his inner strength is sufficient, one day continues the series of teachers of this line.

However, this indissoluble spiritual link does not mean that the chela cannot also sit at the feet of other teachers who, in the absence of his root guru, can help him on his way. There is no competition between real gurus, just as there can be no competition between different aspects of the truth. No single teacher can exhaust all aspects of the truth or of ultimate reality. And even if this were possible, each teacher would still teach his own individual way to the ultimate goal, a path the specific method of which is only binding on that chela who has received empowerment to teach and has been called to continue the succession in that line of gurus.

But not every chela, however hard he may try, possesses such a degree of inner kinship with his guru as to be capable of succeeding him as a teacher. And since the degree of realization depends not only on one's harmonization with the guru, but also on the character and abilities of the disciple, a guru cannot help every one of his chelas to an equal degree. When people come to him as seekers, he will not even try to convey his own thoughts to them; he will rather endeavor to enter into their thoughts and feelings, so as to have a clear idea of where they stand, and then to help them find the approach and the path appropriate to them. If need be, he will send seekers to teachers of other schools, if they can be helped better in this way. For though the supreme goal of all Buddhist schools is the same, the ways and methods of reaching it are in part very different, because they are adapted to suit different abilities and characters.

On the other hand, one should consider that, even though all these paths lead to the same goal, it would be foolish to change from one method to another before exhausting all the possibilities of the one. It would be still more foolish to practice different methods simultaneously, or even to go at one and the same time to two or more different gurus. One should have come to know the various methods *before* entering into a chelaship, but once the decision has been taken it is necessary to follow consistently along the chosen path, unless this should prove not to lead one to the goal. In such a case we should follow the example of the Buddha, who left both his teachers when he realized that their methods did not lead to the liberation he was seeking.

The bond linking guru and chela is *maitrī*. Through this, the guru recognizes the chela's potentialities as well as the hindering forces of established habits that constitute his karma. For the chela, *maitrī* makes possible a trustful opening up without reservation or limitation, with a corresponding removal of prejudices, self-reference, and negativism. By thus surrendering himself he can become heir to a spiritual tradition that has been passed down through many generations and has continually developed, and as he takes hold of it there is gradually accomplished in him a continuous process of transformation of what at first seemed strange into his own—a process similar to that of taking in food, in which the alien substance of the nutriments is first resolved into its elements and then, by assimilation, built into the substance of the body itself. But many earnest seekers today, who are concerned with the religious heritage of mankind, forget that in the process of "assimilation," when that which can be assimilated has been transformed, what is left must be eliminated. This process is not an intellectual one, but an organic or psychic one. It is a process of growth that continues for long periods, in which "one's own" is not assimilated to the "alien," but the originally alien receives, through mental adaptation and inward experience, a unique and individual character of its own.

I was once asked, "Do you regard the reincarnation of your former guru as your present teacher?" I replied, "Would you, having been married in a previous life, regard the reincarnation of a woman from one of your past lives as your wife today?" This counterquestion should make the position clear: just as a marriage contract or a personal relationship from a previous existence cannot retain its validity in this life, since the former partners have changed according to their own inner laws of being (even though certain basic elements remain the same, and the common feeling of a deeper affinity leaves its traces in the form of a spiritual or emotional kinship), so too the guru in his new incarnation cannot occupy the same position toward his former chela for the simple reason that the latter in the course of his own development has ripened the very seed that the guru once sowed in him, so that he is now in a position to offer its fruits in gratitude and loving remembrance to his former teacher.

But whether it is old or new, the inner relation between guru and chela remains, even if their outward roles may appear to have been reversed. Again and again they will meet until the tasks of both have been fulfilled—until both have become one in that supreme light that is the origin and goal of both, and that has joined them through many births and deaths.

When I look back now over the long path of my life, it was always that light that guided me. I see my life's path winding through a wide and varied landscape that is dominated by a mighty river—the river of the spiritual tradition that has flowed without beginning or end through the thousands of years of human life and striving. It embodies the experiences of innumerable generations of people whom religion has inspired: seers and singers, poets and thinkers, artists and scholars, saints and sinners. The sources of this river are the Enlightened Ones who ever and anon take shape among humanity, as for instance Śākyamuni Buddha, whose message was of such universal significance that even after two and a half thousand years we have still not exhausted the depth of its content and the multiplicity of its forms of expression or of its ways of realization. To stand within such a tradition is an obligation, and anyone who denies it in order to go his own way places himself outside the ranks of the spiritual succession of guru and chela, which has come down to us in an unbroken chain and which conveys spiritual authority to us. It is on this that the import of every initiation reposes, which should only be given to those who have fully understood this and who accept this tradition as an obligation.

However, to be a member of such a tradition does not mean that one must take over uncritically all conceptions, practices, and methods that had their importance and value in the past, but that are now merely of historical interest. In the tradition of our order we combine the streams of the three great *yānas* of Buddhism. All their schools have contributed valuable ideas to us, but in the course of the centuries they have remained stuck at particular points of development. And when today they try to jump over their own shadows, they often end up in an extreme form of Western-style intellectualism with a relativization of all values. This leads to the loss of any goal and, as a result, of all sense of responsibility or of ethics. Thus it can come about that even quite extreme excesses can be praised and glorified as "spontaneous actions."

The spontaneity of selfless action and the automatic reaction of an average person are never the same thing. The latter is really behaving like an animal that follows its instinct without the possibility of making a free decision. But spontaneity means that a person has developed an ego and then transcends its limitations. Consciousness needs a focal point in order to be effective. It is this focal point that we call "I" or "self." But this focal point changes position every moment, and since this fact is not realized, the "ego-illusion" arises, which leads us into the senseless attempt to fix the momentary focus, or even to claim that several different focal points are identical.

A guru in the West must be able to enter mentally into the situation as well as the mental and cultural background of his Western pupil. He must lead the pupil to the core, not to the various incrustations that have grown around this. For Buddhism, in its home territories, has no more remained free of incrustations than has European Christianity. Prayers and invocations, poetical descriptions of transcendental fields and beings are scarcely able to convey to a present-day person the inward meaning of a *sādhana,* the meaning which alone leads to the experiencing of the symbolism and the understanding of the psychic processes and of the ineffable spiritual reality.

Sādhanas and other Tantric texts are available today in numerous translations. Since they are often just literally translated, they rarely convey any deeper understanding. They get lost in minute details in which all intuition is suffocated, and thereby block the way for Western man—who has just begun to shake himself free from the dogmatism and scholasticism of the Christian churches with their narrow puritanism—so that he is prevented from coming to the experience of Buddhist universality and profundity of consciousness.

For this reason a guru who feels responsibility for his pupils will always hesitate to present Tantric *sādhanas* schematically, because every one of them would require a whole book of explanations and references, such as my own book *The Foundations of Tibetan Mysticism,* which is meant merely as an *introduction* to the *mantra* OṂ, MANI PADME HŪṂ.

Furthermore, consideration should be given to the fact that a Western chela should not be initiated into the *sādhanas* without a sufficiently long and thorough period of preparation, because people's overstimulation of senses in the sphere of Western civilization is such that both sense perception and imagination are untrained, and therefore usually hard to appeal to and incapable of properly functioning, so that a preliminary period of refresher practice needs to be introduced to begin with. And parallel to this there should be a properly guided introductory course in the essentials of the Dharma, without which all meditative training is directionless and therefore wasted. The pupil must also learn to keep wide awake and clearly aware by continually reviewing his body, his feelings and sensations, his perceptions and understandings, as well as his voluntary and instinctive tendencies. He must also develop the four "Illimitables": love, compassion, sympathetic joy, and ego-free impartiality, joined with equanimity toward everything that concerns himself, in order, on the bodhisattva path, increasingly to dissolve greed, hatred, and delusion by the practice of the *pāramitās*. Above all, he must learn to distinguish between the "finger pointing at the moon" and the "moon" itself, he must learn to get free of all that is formal, purely intellectual, dogmatic, or dated, as well as all that is mere routine. It is just as much the task of the guru to assist the pupil in these things as it is his task to liberate him from his egocentricity, vanity, and egoistic vulnerability.

During this phase the guru will for some time be a standing challenge to his chela, who, as long as he does not see through his own ego, will feel misunderstood and hurt, and only those who really do have a call can stand this strict process of purification. It cannot be expected at all, or only to a limited extent, of the others. Thus it was that Marpa let only his most gifted pupil, Milarepa, painfully feel his inadequacy by continually destroying the values he had just painstakingly created, by refusing to recognize his greatest achievements, and by continually postponing the longed-for initiation, thus bringing him at last to abandon all egocentricity, egoism, all seeking of rewards, and all illusions about having gained any merit. In the same way the guru will bring down his most gifted chela from the dreamy heights of self-glorification to the reality of the here and now and will stretch him to the limit of his capabilities, in order to "let the gold shine forth purified from dross in the fire of devotion." But whatever trials and tasks he gives him are all for the purpose of furthering the inner process of maturation. And behind all the harshness is concealed the love of the guru for his chela, with whom he shares all experiences and sufferings.

It is the tragedy of our time that just when the West has to a certain extent overcome its prejudices against the Vajrayāna and its methods, a number of self-styled "gurus" of Eastern and Western origin have busily set about fabricating a parody of the ancient Tantric tradition with pseudoscientific claims. Some of them turn *mantras* into mechanical aids in a misunderstood psychiatric therapy that is void of any sensible content or of any kind of religious values. Other naive advocates of Eastern teachings, with no understanding of the Western mentality, are trying to import their doctrines into the West while forgetting to supply the necessary conditions to provide Western pupils with a real understanding of Eastern thought and feeling, so that they do not do violence to their common sense or even throw overboard the genuine values of their own culture. But the worst of all is that the invasion of the West by hordes of pseudogurus doing business with all modern forms of advertising has led to such a decline in all religious and spiritual values that even the good work done by serious exponents of Eastern culture is in danger of being misunderstood and rejected by all right-thinking people.

Let it once more be pointed out here that the practice found in many places today of conveying Tantric *sādhanas* and the appropriate *abhiṣeka* in a sort of "mass initiation" to a crowd of insufficiently prepared aspirants is in conflict with the old traditions, and above all with the essence of a true initiation. A conscientious guru will, before granting a *dīkṣa** (Tib. *lung*), or, still more, an *abhiṣeka,* subject his chela to a long preparation and will test him seriously before then giving him individually the particular *sādhana* that corresponds to his stage of development and his situation. Just as a doctor does not give all his patients the same medicine, and even with the same disease must give different doses, so too a guru will not prescribe the same meditation method for all his pupils, but will, after a suitable "diagnosis," give each one the practice suited to his particular character and present state of mind.

In other words, the meditative practice conveyed to the chela must be one that sets him going *in the right direction*. It should not only hold his attention (*smṛti*), but also fill him with inspiration (*prīti*), through which his energy (*vīrya*) is activated and a dynamic, spontaneous concentration is produced. This, in contrast to the concentration we achieve by willpower (in which we continually

*Consecration, induction into a religious observance or practice.

have to guard against disturbing interruptions), does not create a condition of continual defense and delimitation, but produces a positive turning toward a lofty goal that moves us in the depths of our being and attracts us irresistibly. This goal is the realization of buddhahood, which is the realization of our human and universal wholeness in the focal point of our individuality; this can only be experienced by us through the idea of that human being who became whole, perfect, fully awakened, and conscious of his universality—who found his visible expression in the noble and yet so humanly close figure of the Buddha, and whose image the chela intuitively perceives in the figure of his guru.

In order to cover exhaustively all the qualities and experiential possibilities of the mind-created form of the Buddha and the guru, a visible, pictorial-schematic presentation of the inner content of this figure is necessary, in the spectrumlike, concentrically arranged projection of a *maṇḍala,* in which all the qualities belonging to this figure (which are at the same time the constituents of our own consciousness) appear in visible, graspable form. But this presupposes that the chela—as was stressed above—must first be familiar with the spiritual landscape of Buddhism. Otherwise he is like a wanderer who, without any knowledge of the terrain or of the map, stumbles around the countryside blindly and aimlessly. If he is lucky, he may find somewhere that suits him—if not, he has lost his chance. Accordingly, the guru always puts the *conveyance of knowledge* first, because *sādhanas* undertaken without knowledge regularly lead one astray; thus the uninitiated, who only works from books, or the ignorant treading the path without a master is always in peril of getting more and more involved in his own ideas and imaginings instead of getting free.

If a chela is accepted by a guru, he has to approach the teacher with *śraddhā* and *bhakti* (trustful openness and devotion): these are two basic conditions without which spiritual guidance is impossible. It is just here that many Western chelas make it hard for themselves, because they cannot bring themselves to bow to their teacher, and become upset when their prejudices and opinions are criticized. Even when they profess to love the teacher, they defend *their* position and maintain *their* standpoint.

But chelaship demands a "beginner's mind," starting from the knowledge that one is now entering a territory one knows nothing about, and where, just as on a climbing expedition or when traveling through unknown and dangerous country, one has to entrust oneself to an experienced guide. The guru here becomes increasingly a model in the literal sense, on whom one models oneself. That such a procedure is only possible where there already exists an inner kinship between master and disciple, and when they are linked by a bond of loving affection, is evident. Only then is it possible, for example, for the beginner's meditation to move not in some realm of abstraction, but for his development of visions to come to life because the chela projects the image of his guru—in whom, for him, the essence of all buddhahood and bodhisattvahood is revealed—into the visions he perceives of divine figures of buddhas and bodhisattvas. Only in this way will he be able to overcome the hardships of the long and dangerous journey without plunging into abysses of despair when he has to go through the preparatory schooling without which any *sādhana* would fail of its purpose and had better not be given. So he must subject himself to a training of his imaginative powers, he must learn to find inner peace of mind (*śamatha*) and intuitive insight into the essence of things (*vipaśyanā*). In this way he purifies his mind and learns to direct it toward the goal he is aiming at, and so he becomes ripe for the bestowal of the *abhiṣeka*.

It seems to be another feature of our time that Western people, even in the realm of the spirit, think in terms of quantity and not quality. Thus many Western meditation enthusiasts show a tendency to "collect" as many different meditation practices and *sādhanas* as possible, instead of making a single one the leading theme of their life. Their minds are not capable of sticking with one thing for long. Their minds are restless and thus always on the lookout to pick up something new, to try something different "just once in a while." But we should not bother so much about how many different meditation methods we *could* try. The sole point is the intensity with which one practices in the once chosen direction. Then, even if we have received only one initiation and practice only one *sādhana*, we have—if we succeed in opening up completely—received all the *abhiṣekas*. Whoever meditates with devotion and an open mind or—as Suzuki Rōshi so fittingly called it—with a "beginner's mind," even in the simplest possible form, will attain to a breakthrough. But anyone who simultaneously follows different methods, now this, now that, and now all together, is blocking his own path and merely marking time.

It is even worse if someone, having collected various "initiations," imagines himself to be somebody special. The inflated ego then prevents any progress on the path and traps him in more and more inextricable entanglements. We should therefore always bear in mind that an *abhiṣeka* is something precious, and take good care not to increase still further the present-day inflationary offer of initiations. Meditation in the Vajrayāna demands persistence from the chela. Even in times when for long periods "nothing happens," the *sādhana* must be constantly at work in all that we do. For one cannot take up a meditation today and forget it for a while tomorrow with the intention of trying it again sometime: the thread is then broken and can scarcely be picked up again.

As we have already made clear, the guru-chela relation depends on a sublime spiritual elective affinity through which master and disciple find each other and remain bound together for life. From this already preexisting kinship in thinking and feeling, and the bond of *maitrī* that develops from it, the chela recognizes in the guru the model he must follow. The process thus initiated is comparable to the unfoldment of a child into a mature and well developed personality.

For this very reason it becomes clear that chelaship with a guru does not mean the renunciation of personal responsibility and thought. One goes to a guru in order to be faced with a challenge and trained in responsibility, not in order to get rid of one's own thoughts and feelings, but rather to learn to subject these to a watchful and severe testing against the word of the guru. For this reason it is quite unnecessary to defend one's own point of view to one's guru. A true guru is not concerned with imposing conformity on thoughts and feelings. He wants to arouse personal recognition and experience in the chela—not to teach him but to inspire him. But he also wants to liberate his chela from the attachment to opinions, prejudices, and dogmas—and this is often a painful process.

In the series of gurus of the tradition of our order, *siddhas* and masters such as Tilopa, Naropa, Marpa, and Milarepa occupy a special position. Thus Milarepa, although he lived a celibate life, never belonged to the *bhikṣu-sangha* or wore its robes. His guru Marpa, one of Tibet's greatest lamas, who was married and had children, was himself the pupil of the *mahāsiddha* Naropa, who had once been one of the leading lights at the Buddhist university of Vikramaśīla, a Brahmin by birth, and as a *mahāpaṇḍita* once an honored member of the *bhikṣu-sangha*. But in spite of his learning and his virtuous life he was unable to realize the goal of enlightenment. When he met the guru Tilopa, a wandering yogi and teacher of the *mahāmudrā* doctrine, who had gained liberation, Naropa abandoned his high office and his monkish robe in order to follow the *siddha* and receive initiation into the *mahāmudrā* doctrine.

Tilopa taught him: "Where the mind has no place where it can stop (and be delimited), there the *mahāmudrā* is present. By cultivating such an attitude one will achieve supreme enlightenment." In other words, *mahāmudrā* is the universal attitude of mind which by nature is unlimited and all-embracing, or as Tilopa put it: "The treasure house of original mind is free from selfish passions and shines like the unlimited heaven." Under Tilopa's guidance, Naropa trod the path of spontaneous experiencing and realization of the universal depth-consciousness, which for him had been buried under mountains of scholastic learning, abstract philosophical speculations, hair-splitting arguments, and monkish rules, according to which virtue was not the product of higher knowledge but the result of mere denial. This self-satisfaction with acquired negative virtues was the greatest obstacle on the path to enlightenment for the scholarly Naropa, more so than all possible passions, which through insight into the true nature of things could be transformed and sublimated into forces working for liberation.

It is only in this context that the seemingly paradoxical saying of Tilopa's, "The true nature of the passions has revealed itself as the sublime knowledge of liberation," makes sense. For only a person who is capable of great passions can perform great, indeed the greatest, tasks and finally attain to perfection in the realm of the spirit. Only someone who, like Milarepa, has gone through the fire of suffering and despair is capable of reaching the supreme goal within one lifetime.

The biographies of Naropa, Marpa, and Milarepa let us see the essentials in the guru-chela relation. The passing on of information in the sense of a particular teaching tradition plays here only a subordinate role. The guru sees his task rather as enabling the chela to reduce his egocentricity, to free himself from all vanities, from feeling hurt and insulted, from his dependence on praise and blame. He lets him see the hollowness of a morality that has not matured in life, and confronts him with the opinions, prejudices, and creeds that he has merely taken over from others. He displays the whole gamut of his emotions to him, so that he can learn to open up without prejudice in order to come to an immediate insight that is not falsified by any dogmatism.

Further, the chela experiences in his link with the person of the guru a sense of being one in an unbroken chain of spiritual transmission reaching from Śākyamuni Buddha to himself, which lays on him the obligation to commit all his forces to the gaining of the supreme goal of enlightenment. In the guru there is embodied for him the whole chain of those who passed on and kept alive the sacred tradition, generation after generation, for thousands of years, just as Śākyamuni Buddha himself stands for the incalculable number of all the Enlightened Ones who preceded him, and who have followed and will follow him.

Just as the guru stands on the shoulders of his predecessors, so too the chela stands on his guru's shoulders with the obligation to assimilate and transform the inspiration he has received from his guru by his own experience until it becomes an expression of his inner nature, in which, high above all verbal knowledge and all scholasticism, the sublime spirit of the guru is resurrected in fresh form. Only in this way can it come about that the chela becomes a guru, and the guru, on a higher level, again becomes a chela, and that in this living interplay the profoundest bond between guru and chela seeks its expression, remaining always capable of a continual further elevation, until the ineffable has been accomplished and the mighty task has been done.

I have frequently been asked whether it is really necessary to have a guru. No, it is not absolutely indispensable, but very much to be desired. There are people who are capable of penetrating to the depths and discovering everything afresh for themselves that others have to struggle to acquire painfully by methodical learning under the guidance of experienced teachers. But such people are rare exceptions. And even in their case there is little sense in trying to rediscover everything that generations of wise men, saints, and thinkers have already found out. Only very few of these exceptional individuals would in such conditions gain their self-set goal in a single lifetime and be able to realize what they are striving for. For man does not live in a historyless space. We are all heirs of those who lived before us. But this knowledge involves the obligation to make what we have inherited entirely our own, in order to let it come alive within us through experiencing from example and afresh. For it is only what we ourselves have experienced and come to know that can initiate a process of transformation—never what we have taken over for the sake of a sacred tradition.

7 | *The Introspective Paths in Buddhism and Their Significance for Humanity Today*

For many centuries people in the West had almost totally forgotten what is today embraced by the term "meditation." And then suddenly, in the last decades, the book market of Europe and America has been flooded with a spate of works dealing with this subject, as a result of which meditation has become almost fashionable. Since no living traditions survived in the West (apart from the spiritual exercises of Ignatius Loyola), there was at first an indiscriminate grasping at the written accounts of Eastern methods, which—detached from their religious and cultural background—were then interpreted according to the views of various authors, often being changed in the process and advocated like goods on the market. On the basis of such constructions, other authors then developed their own homemade methods "on the basis of personal experience," and these were put before the public as "being fully adapted to the needs of Western people." But even a cursory glance shows that most of these authors lacked any meditative experience: they simply invented systems that often led those who followed them into states of dependence instead of to liberty in responsibility.

If we want to learn from the meditation systems that exist in the East today, we must first of all be clear about one thing: what is understood in the West today by "meditation" includes many different things, a variety of quite different practices that, starting from different religious and cultural assumptions, aim in part at mutually contradictory goals. But since these methods were developed depending on a particular worldview as a starting point and with a particular goal in mind, simply to take them over makes no sense if one's own path, which is conditioned by different religious and philosophical ideas, aims at a different goal. And even if there is agreement with the direction of the chosen meditation technique, even then the guru must allow for variations depending on the individual needs, and the starting point, of the chela.

If one has once understood this, it can be realized that it is impossible to give generalized meditation instruction to groups or even to people with whom one has no personal contact, and whose mental attitude and psychic potential are more or less unknown to one. Thus, meditation training is always something very individual, and can and should according to the Buddhist tradition—and indeed the general Eastern tradition—only be done within the narrow confines of the guru-chela relationship.

This fact was taken into account even as early as the tradition of the Pali canon, from which we see that not every form of meditation is considered suitable for everybody. Here already six types of people are distinguished, for whom six different specific ways of practice are recommended.

In the Mahāyāna and Vajrayāna the paths of meditative practice were further refined, so that the guru could find a "made-to-measure" type of practice for each one of his pupils. This presupposes that the spiritual teacher first carefully investigates the capacities and inclinations of his pupil, in order to provide an appropriate way for him to follow, step by step. But such a guidance can never be given through a fixed program that follows a ready-made scheme. For the chela may at any stage of development have extraordinary experiences and can fall into serious psychopathological fantasies or confused states that the guru must recognize and avert in time, and this can only take place in the context of close personal contact and living together. It is only under such conditions that the guru can lovingly encourage his pupil by his own example and exemplary life, so that the pupil can himself develop his positive qualities and reduce or transform the negative ones without the dynamism of creative meditation being stifled by schematization and regimentation.

Since, as we saw, the methods and goal of a meditation are so largely determined by the goal aimed at, it is only honorable to point out to all who seek to be initiated into meditation that the path we teach can only be that of *Buddhist* meditation. If a person is prepared by his own decision to tread this path, he should first be asked what brought him to Buddhism, and what especially interests him about the Dharma. From the answers to these questions the first pointers can be derived for initiating the meditation practice. For those who are impressed and attracted by the great mystical visions of the Vajrayāna must necessarily be guided differently from those who are attracted by the consistency of Buddhist logic, or by the nobility of the Four Immeasurable States (*brahmavihāras*), or by the profound humanity and goodness of a bodhisattva or a buddha.

Doubtless it would be ideal if one could introduce, once for all, a meditative training sufficiently complex to embrace all aspects. But any such integrative effort would at once fail, because every person who comes to us is a being with a history of its own. He himself presents us with the object that inspires him and that he can learn to love. Choosing this and making it the starting point for his meditation work is a psychological necessity, because only such an object is capable of helping him over periods when he despairs, when his meditation makes no progress, and when—still in the grip of a false ambition to achieve—he falls into depression.

The common starting point of all Buddhist meditation is the experiential insight that man's experience of suffering is rooted in his "I am" illusion. It is through this that man, ignorant of the truth, separates himself from his fellow beings as well as from the sources of the greater life, thereby continually building bigger and bigger walls and barriers around himself, which it is the task of meditation practice to tear down. There are two possible ways to achieve this breakthrough and to restore the unity of our consciousness. One is the path of asceticism and denial of the world, according to which the world is rejected as a mere illusion and thus devalued and our individuality is dissolved in the uncreated ground of all being. The second way leads us through a dynamic development of our thinking, feeling, and acting to the unfolding of dedication and love, of shared sorrow with the sufferings of others and shared joy with their happiness, and, furthermore, to an affirmation of reality while recognizing all individual values in their constant mutability. For it is this mutability that makes it possible for us to experience the transparency and so too the transcending of the individuality, which in its dynamism is subjected to continuous change and, while not staying the same for a single instant, can yet be experienced continuously as the point of intersection and focus of all the rays of power of the universe. In this experience the opposition between *saṃsāra* and *nirvāṇa* is resolved. We come to see that the very same world that appears to the unenlightened mind as *saṃsāra* is experienced by the enlightened mind as *nirvāṇa*.

It has frequently been objected that the aim of Buddhist meditation is to let man sink back into a state of uncreatedness, that it seeks a regression into the unconscious and thus a destruction of the individual. The Buddha himself had to defend himself against this view:

> Here, monks, a monk has got rid of the conceit "I am," cut it off at the roots . . . so that it cannot grow again. . . . Monks, when a monk's mind is freed thus, the *devas*, those with Indra, Brahmā, and Pajāpati, do not succeed in their search if they think: "This is the consciousness attached to a Tathāgata." And why? I say that even in this life a Tathāgata is untraceable. And because I speak thus and teach thus, there are some *samaṇas* [wandering ascetics] and Brahmins who misrepresent me untruly, vainly, falsely, and not in accordance with fact: "The *samaṇa* Gotama is a nihilist, he teaches the cutting off, the destruction, the nonexistence of an existing entity." But this is what I am not and what I do not teach, of which these worthy *samaṇas* and Brahmins accuse me untruly, vainly, falsely, and not in accordance with fact. What I formerly taught and teach now is suffering and the cessation of suffering. (*Majjhima Nikāya* 22, *Alagaddūpama Sutta*)

But the overcoming of suffering and, with it, the extinction of greed, hatred, and delusion is the breakthrough to awakening and enlightenment, by which the components of the personality that cause us to experience the world as *saṃsāra* become transformed into the elements of the personality of a fully enlightened one. The sole purpose of Buddhist meditation is to initiate and develop this process, which effects a transformation of the entire human personality through continually watchful clear presence of mind and the unfolding of all the powers vested in us, while at the same time developing the limitless potentialities of consciousness, whereby we become masters of our own life and are able to break through to enlightenment.

And so in meditation we sow the seed of liberation, and thereby form here and now the bodies of future perfection according to the creative image of our highest ideals. But we do not cling to the past, which in any case we cannot change. We are people of our time, whose thinking and feeling bears the stamp of an experiential world that people of past ages—however highly spiritual in their development—simply did not know. And whereas the laws of existence, both within and without, always remain the same, many things have decisively changed in our surroundings.

Thus, in this age of space travel, atomic science, computer techniques, and massive industrialization, our worldview is different from that of people in antiquity or the Middle Ages. Yet most of the meditation methods with which people of today are confronted were developed hundreds or thousands of years ago. It is true that they are essentially based on principles that are common to all mankind and timeless, because the basic structure of the human psyche has hardly changed. But on the periphery of our consciousness many things have changed, so that we cannot today simply take over unseen the methods of former times if we do not want to close down altogether on critical thought. Western man has needed a long time to get free of the dogmatism and scholasticism of the Middle Ages, and just as long to escape the bonds of puritanism of the succeeding centuries. He would simply block his path to experiencing the universality, depth of consciousness, and liberty that are basic to Buddhism if he were to take over uncritically certain methods that were justified in past ages, which had entirely different social structures and worldview models.

Only a few decades ago I was able to observe how the Tibetans possessed a profoundly trustful faith (*śraddhā*, Tib. *dam-tshig*) that made them capable of almost limitless devotion. They still lived at that time in a magical world that was not mechanical and soulless, but penetrated by spirit. Because of this worldview they had direct access to the depths of their own consciousness, such as we can only strive to attain by the indirect path of intellectual-psychological understanding. For the wheel of time cannot be turned back, and thus we cannot return to the magical world by negation of our mental state of consciousness.

For us, there is only a progression to a wholeness that must be gained by continual integration, in which the many dimensions of the depth-consciousness (in which that world of magic also has its place) come to be experienced. If we, as people of our time, want to make use of the possibilities of the Buddhist Vajrayāna, our line of approach must go first through learning to appreciate the inner meaning of the basic symbols and visions of this school; we should pay less attention to prayers, invocations, and poetic descriptions of transcendental landscapes and beings such as visions of hells and heavens. Many things occurred in medieval Buddhism that are comparable to medieval Christianity: the simplicity and immediacy of the beginning (as we still find it, for instance, in the *Sādhanamālā*) became overgrown with numerous nonessential and partly misleading details, as well as with certain primitive ideas born of fear or wishful thinking.

There thus arose schematic meditation procedures, which accordingly soon became sterile, in which the visionary development was increasingly suffocated under a host of prayers that were read off. Some of these prayers, indeed, were not even understood. Such an uncomprehending rattling off of prayers, like their mechanical repetition a hundred thousand times, leads at best to relaxation through self-hypnosis, but never to the living experience of that profound reality that has nothing to do with pious words and emotional outbursts.

Accordingly, we need to reveal the kernel of the *sādhanas*, freed from all useless ballast. And then we shall find that the images are just as effective today as they ever were, especially if the pupil is trained from the very beginning to remind himself that all visions we produce in meditation (which are therefore called *bhāvanā*, which means "making to become") are not some kind of "divine revelations of ultimate reality," but have their origin in the mind and psyche of the meditator. Already in the *Mahāyāna-Śraddhotpāda-Śāstra* it says, "When pupils have visions of gods, bodhisattvas, and tathāgatas, surrounded by heavenly glory, they should remember that these are all *mind-made*."

And yet, these mind-made beings are not unreal. Their reality consists in the fact that they release active forces within us that not only initiate the process of transformation, but continually stimulate it. They resemble works of art that are born from the profoundest experiences of the human spirit and which, even if they do not last and possess no objective existence, still contain symbols whose continually recurring forms are pointers and inspirers toward the highest perfection—enlightenment.

If we want to make the Vajrayāna and its meditation methods useful for our times, we must beware of approaching them purely intellectually and losing ourselves in philosophical-metaphysical speculations, schematic iconographies, and mystifying theorems. The practice of Vajrayāna requires, over and above any intellectual activity, a continuous meditative training in the original *sādhanas*, together with the sacred rite of initiation, through which the joint work of guru and chela becomes a living and dynamic process of mental development. But, in order that this process may be saved from stagnation, we must continually remind ourselves that the Tantras repeatedly warn against two extremes: we should neither regard the visions of the higher states of consciousness as "ultimate reality"—which would lead to our becoming attached to them, and so stopping halfway—nor should we deny all reality to such visions on the grounds that they are *merely* mind-made. In the latter case we would fail to recognize the decisive role played by our consciousness and its potential capabilities, and thus deprive ourselves of a valuable aid on our path.

Meditation, as a state of increased awareness, is directed both inward and outward. It should therefore be used not as a way of escape from the world, but solely as a means by which to penetrate deeper into the essence of things and into our own nature. Only in this way can it reunite the inner and outer worlds without our imagining that we have to give up the one for the sake of the other. In this way we shall succeed in experiencing wisdom and compassion as a single whole that are as inseparable as is the flame with light and warmth.

The Buddha gained his enlightenment sitting under the Bodhi Tree. But it would be wrong to suppose that one can gain enlightenment merely by "sitting." Of course it is a good thing to learn to sit properly as a beginner in meditation—to sit in a position that permits us to dwell for a long time over the object of our meditation without pain and the distraction it causes. But the important thing is not the sitting itself, but the original impulse in the right direction or the directing content, which not only seizes our attention (*smṛti*), but also fills us with inspiration (*prīti*), as a result of which a natural state of concentration spontaneously comes about. People today in the West, especially in the big industrialized countries, lack the capacity for genuine devotion (*bhakti*), which is a basic requirement for meditative absorption. Without this, all meditation gets stuck in abstraction. And here it is that the example of the Buddha, the Enlightened One, presents itself as a living, experienceable, actual reality, which transforms and shapes us after its internal image.

But meditation training should not only make use of one-sidedly chosen elements of our minds, it should be borne forward simultaneously on various levels of consciousness. Thus, beside the study of Buddhist texts and the Tantric tradition, it is necessary to develop to the full *clear awareness* as well as the creative faculty of the *imagination*. It is only when these conditions have been met that the initiation into a *sādhana* has any point. Without such preparatory schooling, any *abhiṣeka* would fail of its purpose, and so ought not to be given.

Just these two things, clear awareness and the development of the imagination, are all the more important for people today, because everything conspires, on the one hand, by overstimulation continually to hinder people in achieving a clear and full awareness of the present, and on the other hand to rob them of the ability to use their imagination creatively. Even a child is deprived of the chance to develop its imagination because it is given a perfect toy that in every case imitates the so-called real world. And further, from an early age the child is hampered by radio and television in trying to develop its own imagination.

In my books I have always tried to present these problems in the form of a multicolored mosaic containing partly elements from the past, partly those from the present. But I was always well aware of the dangers of such an undertaking. On the other hand, this procedure also had a positive side. If one only gives hints and suggestions, this prevents others from turning a detailed description into a "scheme valid for all time." And it is precisely on the inward path that one of the greatest dangers is that of schematically fixing meditation instructions. As a warning example we might mention certain aberrations in the presentation of the *satipaṭṭhāna* (mindfulness) practice, in which the last remnant of the possibility of spontaneous experience is shattered with the bludgeon of analytical demolition techniques.

Whoever is serious about meditation will assuredly find his spiritual teacher who will provide him with the material and the tools. He will also teach and inspire him to make such use of these that he finds a creative joy in his efforts on the path of self-discovery. In this way—inspired by a genuine guru-chela relationship—he will grasp the full meaning of the old doctrine of the Buddhist Vajrayāna, which never said, "Here is the answer (or: the theory). Just train your mind to accept and believe it!" but which challenged the pupil: "Here is the problem, and here are the tools. Work out the solution for yourself!"

Within this process of purification and developing of awareness, the choice of *sādhana* for each chela is of crucial importance. If today translations of Tantric texts are published all over the place and *sādhanas* are freely available to anyone and everyone, this is an undesirable state of affairs that causes more confusion and misunderstandings than it clears up. The run-of-the-mill scholars who tackle such translations are no more aware of their responsibilities than those groups who hand out *sādhanas* like sweets to everyone without any previous individual introduction, and without the preliminary exercises that, at least in medieval India, were never written down but passed on orally.

When Evans-Wentz published certain Buddhist Tantric texts in his day, he at least tried to put the reader on the right track and to inspire him with a certain respect for the esoteric content of these writings. And so the short texts selected by him as well as the basic parts of the *Bardo Thödol* can be recommended. But the biographies of Naropa and Padmasambhava and the translations of early Sanskrit Tantras (such as the *Hevajra* and *Guhyasamāja Tantras*) are scarcely of any use without a knowledge of the symbolic language and apart from meditative practice under an experienced guru.

One of the greatest mistakes of our time is to suppose that the *sādhanas* have existed for thousands of years unchanged. Only the basic forms were created by the great masters of the past, and these were then varied by generations of teachers who followed them, right down to recent times. Here the saying is true: "The master can wisely break the form at the right time"—in order to create the variations necessary for his chela.

What has been shown so far makes it clear that without devotion, without inspiration, and without spontaneity meditation turns into mere self-stupefaction and self-deception, and regularly degenerates into a routine activity. But devotion that fills us with enthusiasm and strength can only ripen in a person who is encouraged to aim at a worthwhile and lofty goal by *knowledge*. For that reason all training in Buddhist meditation must be preceded by an intensive study of the Buddha-Dharma, though this must not become stuck in scholasticism whose dry intellectualism and schematism can easily maneuver the student into a false feeling of satisfaction, the result of which—assuming that he subsequently meditates at all—lets him slip into a schematic system of meditation that is opposed to all genuine experience. But from an absorption in the Buddha's teaching born of consideration and reflection, the chela will develop an enthusiasm for a particular aspect of the Dharma that inspires him and so—from the concentration naturally arising in a mind that is fascinated—becomes the object of his meditative attention.

The collection and concentration of all our inner powers in a suitable focal point is the prerequisite for all meditative work. This fact, owing to a misunderstanding of the situation, has often led to the false interpretation whereby the simple process of concentration is equated with meditation, although the difference ought to be obvious. A simple example will make this clear. Every bookkeeper, sitting over his figures, reckonings, and calculations, is concentrating, but he is certainly not meditating. In fact, concentration and meditation are so totally different, that it often happens that our very wish to be able to concentrate during meditation on some object becomes a hindrance by assuming a compulsive character.

Meditation, in the sense of the Buddha's teaching, is actually based on a letting go of both desire and aversion, as a result of which that inner calm (Skt. *praśrabdhi,* Pali *passaddhi*) arises in us that permits us to observe ourselves and the continuous stream of our thoughts without valuation and without fixation. In this way we offer no opposition to the dynamism working within us, allowing everything to flow freely without being trapped by this or that thought. Thus we see and recognize the play of thought in accordance with reality, namely as a process that cannot be stopped, however hard we try. The only thing we can do is to watch the flashing forth and disappearing of thoughts without paying particular attention to any one of them. For if we turn our attention even for a moment to a specific thought, we at once start a chain of associations that unfolds more and more.

The Buddha and many of his great disciples investigated analytically the process of thought and the course of mental activities and demarcated the importance and the boundaries of thought in order, by breaking through these boundaries in meditative vision to reach a consciousness that is beyond space and time and not accessible to thought, and concerning which, therefore, nothing can be said. In experiencing this "presence of consciousness" we discover a reality that transforms us. Suddenly we are open and transparent, and in us occurs the miracle of the ever renewed beginning.

Some time ago, somebody asked me how one could define meditation briefly. I replied, "Meditation is that possibility through which the individual can become aware of his continual, never broken integration in the universe." The way of meditation is thus the only chance with a hope of success to see through the ego complex and thus to conquer the illusion of a self detached from and independent of the whole. This is something that cannot be brought about by either pious sermons or spiritual admonitions: the process of change started by meditation increasingly brings about the abolition of our attachment to that fictitious "I" that, not recognizing the relativity of its own existence, wants to cut itself off from the universe. In the experience of the interconnection of all life we enter the freedom of a continually, dynamically changing individuality that has become transparent and that—linked up in an endless network of relations—knows itself as the conscious, "present-moment" point of intersection of the universal process of becoming.

By the overcoming of the ego-illusion there develops with no effort on our part a selflessness that is free from any feeling of moral superiority or arrogance. The fellow feeling and compassion (*mahākaruṇā*) that arises from this attitude is a spontaneous, natural expression of solidarity with all life; it is neither an ideologically inflated form of emotionalism nor something undertaken by the command of a God. And so, meditation, when properly undertaken, not only allows us to experience our integration into the whole (without which we would have no existence), it also lets us become aware that, like every sentient being, we are a continually changing focal point, in which the universe becomes conscious of itself in unique fashion.

Such an experiencing of universality and of the uniqueness of individual existence in its continual process of change fills us with a growing sense of responsibility to the whole. It becomes necessary to develop this personality into an ever more perfect instrument of perception, and at the same time of service for the good of all beings. Therefore properly conducted meditation leads neither to "self-destruction" and dissolution into a nebulously conceived "all" or "nothing," nor to a hardening of self that sets the ego in opposition to the whole of life, conceived as the "wholly other," in order to develop through self-absorption a state of indifference to the world we live in. Meditation in the spirit of the Buddha will rather enable us to see all things and all beings in a greater context, in which the triviality of our worldly life suddenly appear as if transformed in a new light, namely as deeply significant aspects of a cosmic play in which we are at one and the same time actors and spectators.

If I here speak of a "cosmic play," this can easily be misinterpreted, because the concept of "play" for many people is connected with ideas such as "arbitrariness," "caprice," and "chance." For them, "playing" is something where one simply lets oneself go, something with neither order nor purpose. A moment's thought, however, would show them that games always follow definite rules. For example, in soccer every player must know the rules exactly and obey them strictly, although he could run around the field freely and do whatever he liked—but if he did, he would disrupt the game and be sent off the field.

In the great universal game the rules are what we call Dharma. Without understanding the Dharma we cannot make full use of our liberty in the game we are all playing. And so, just as even in an improvised play everyone who takes an active part must know what character he is supposed to represent in order to fit into the play and act convincingly, so in the great cosmic play, no one can act his part perfectly unless he has an intuitive perception of the total context and fits his performance into the whole.

Meditation is one of the ways to teach us the part we have to play in this life. It gives us certainty about our starting point, our possibilities of development, our degree of liberty, and also about the responsibility that rests on us. For there can be *no freedom without responsibility*. Perhaps that is why so many people are afraid of liberty, because they are afraid of the responsibility it involves. What they are looking for is often mere lack of restraint, freedom from commitment, irresponsibility, in short a chaotic egoism and an egocentricity that only thinks of the satisfaction of its own confused drives and wishes, which it seeks to satisfy. But liberty is, as Nietzsche said, "insight into necessity"; it is responsible action in conformity with the rules of the "great game" in which we are all involved.

Every meditation that consists of anything more than "just sitting" requires in the Buddhist view intensive preparation. Besides the study of Dharma, the observation of the breathing, of the body, of feelings and mental processes, the contemplation of the form of the Buddha and the Four Divine Abidings (*brahmavihāras*) are just as essential as the moral maturity of the chela. It is only after these preliminaries have been fulfilled that a start should be made on the preparation of the *sādhana* by an introduction into the symbolism, mythology, the direction of the *mantra* and the iconography of the figures that are to be visualized. Only then can one make a start on the meditative vision of the purely mental forms, which are nothing but the forces of the light within us and which at first dwell in our minds only as vague, unclear ideas, but in the course of the meditation develop into effective powers.

The unprepared practicer is very liable to come to grief at the very beginning on the rocks of the hardened ego. And even if he should succeed in avoiding these, there is the danger that he will fall victim to hallucinations as the visions unfold, by taking these self-created images for "objective" reality. And even if he manages to avoid this trap, he runs the further risk in encountering the profound symbolism of the Anuttarayoga Tantra, of misinterpreting the *yab-yum* images sexually instead of experiencing them as an internal process of psychic integration of all the male and female elements of the human personality.

It is quite ridiculous how people in Europe and America today imagine they are capable of practicing the higher Tantric exercises before they have trodden the path of alert mindfulness in the silence of the calmed mind and of the body that is at rest in itself. Westerners encounter many difficulties even in the elementary stages of the Tantra—Kriyā tantra, Carya tantra, and Yoga tantra—because the archetypical forms of the visionary images have not been familiar to them from early childhood, and therefore cannot at first become an *active reality* for them. For the Westerner these are initially only aesthetic or symbolic structures to which he has no living relation. But it is only when these archetypes have become an experienceable reality that they become effective, so that a corresponding *sādhana* can be practiced. The mere repeated reading of *sādhana* texts, as is often practiced today, is quite valueless because it remains merely formal.

A further difficulty for the Westerner is his habit of considering that religious activities should occur only at a particular time of day, or day of the week or month. And this part of the day is seldom or never related to the other occupations of that day. But the Vajrayāna requires the practicer (*sādhaka*) to make every activity a part of his religious practice, which irradiates every minute of the day and whatever he does. Because meditation is not some exceptional condition of human existence. It is rather the development of a mental attitude from which all other activities of life derive their meaning. Even the most everyday actions in kitchen and household are thus placed in the service of a higher reality; in this way an attitude to life is produced by meditation that opens up to life in all its multiplicity, and in this way one's own nature becomes more and more transparent, and therefore brighter and more cheerful, like a room with all the windows open so that it is flooded with warm sunshine.

In this light-filled openness, the nature and presence of Vajrasattva manifests as the quintessence of all the Enlightened Ones, who now, in various different forms, take possession of us more and more, or, as familiar figures, share in our life, feeling, and thinking.

Where this inward familiarity is lacking, meditation turns into an enforced "exercise" with neither inspiration nor spontaneity. It is precisely this that makes it hard for me to speak of the "technique" of meditation, and even to run meditation courses with precise instructions, rules, and exercises that can all too easily lead to a routine that deadens all life. For we can no more teach meditation than we can teach people how to love. And just as every "technique of love" destroys the very thing that love is all about—spontaneity, immediacy, lack of plan and intention, freedom from self—so it is too with meditation if we attempt to describe or teach its "technique."

It cannot be said too often: the role of the guru is to light the flame of inspiration. For only when it has taken total possession of the chela is it possible for everything the guru can present from his own experience for the chela's assistance really turn into fuel for the flame of enlightenment that transforms everything into light and warmth. And so, meditation can only develop into a creative force that is capable of transforming from within and to liberate us, when it has become a *spontaneous* attitude to life in us. And then it will become a creative act from a new attitude, a world renewal or even a world re-creation, through which mental events can be experienced and recognized as active forces.

This spiritual crystallization process of creative productivity is called the "phase of unfolding" (Skt. *sṛṣṭi-krama*, Tib. *bskyed-rim*). But the images and forms made visible by this process would have the effect of reducing everything to a state of spiritual petrifaction if we were not to dissolve these crystallized forms once more into the stream of life and consciousness. This process of "merging" (Skt. *laya-krama*, Tib. *rdzogs-rim*) shows us the nonselfhood (*anātman*), nonabsoluteness, nonsubstantiality, creativity, and revocability of every formation in potential emptiness (*śūnyatā*). Only a person who has learned to employ both methods—unfolding and merging—and who can both create and dissolve again, will be capable of keeping clear of attachment to his own experiences and to the stages he has reached—a danger to which the majority of non-Buddhist mystics succumb.

But whoever has realized that "the actual" is the product of our own action becomes liberated in the most convincing way from the materialistic idea of the world as an "objective" reality standing outside of all relation to a perceiving subject. Thus the experience of these two phases of Tantric meditation is far more convincing than all theoretical and philosophical discussions. And we understand the profound wisdom of a remark by Ludwig Klages: "The vision transforms the viewer; this is clearly in the most extreme contrast to the act of perception, which separates the perceiver from the perceived object and makes him all the more certain of his limited existence-for-himself."

Thus a thing only exists insofar as it acts. Actuality is activity. In this sense the dhyāni buddhas seen in meditation are actual, just as much so as the mind that created them, whereas the Buddha *conceived* as the unique historical personality is in this sense unreal or nonactual. He is only experienced as active when we allow the Dharma that he saw and taught to act on, in, and through us.

Images and symbols that no longer act on people are at best ornamental, or the traditional form of some thought or event belonging to the past. All the great Tantric meditations, with their multitude of symbols, work to counteract this by anticipating the universal goal—the great mystical synthesis and integration that is the perfect enlightenment of a world-saving buddha. Only when the meditator has, with the aid of the symbols, developed the ability to identify with the goal can he give himself over to the multiplicity of other meditative experiences. Just as an archer must take aim at the target and in a sense become one with it in order to be sure of hitting it, so too the meditator must first become clearly aware of his goal and become one with it. This gives his efforts the right direction and inspiration. Then, whatever methods he may later choose—constructive, discriminative, emotional or intellectual, creative or analytical—he will always continue on the right path toward the goal.

Certainly, even visions are not the ultimate. Nor are values or ideas that are liable to be clung to by the intellect. The danger is all the greater because words have a tendency toward narrowing and limitation, whereas the images perceived in genuine vision have a living quality that brings inner maturity. They point, and grow, beyond themselves; they are too immaterial, too "transparent" to become objectified and so to encourage attachment. They can be neither seized upon nor simply described or defined, and thus have a tendency to point away from form to the formless, whereas what is merely thought has the opposite tendency, to become petrified as dogma.

Thus, in Buddhism, symbolism plays a large part from the very beginning. For although Buddhism as a teaching was expressed in clear words, and appeals like no other religion in the world to man's alert intelligence, we must still bear in mind that words have their limits, and that language itself is built up of symbolic concepts, which, even though they have been created over a long period on the basis of general agreement, still only represent a second-degree reality, whereas the *immediate* reality of our personal experience is largely inexpressible in words.

But this does not mean that all verbal knowledge is useless. Within the bounds of its validity it is an important means of communication, and a means that provides our consciousness with a relatively neutral basis, from which we can rise above conventional verbal knowledge in order to explore other dimensions of our experience. It was just this that Buddhism accomplished in the course of time, and in the diamond vehicle this became the principal purpose. The Buddha himself had already said that his teaching was profound and intelligible only to the wise, and that they were wrong who thought the Dharma consisted solely in impressive formulations. He therefore advised all his followers to adopt the way of meditation, the way of experience, of realization and turning within.

But as long as meditation proceeds along the pathways of conventional thought, we are the prisoners of our own thought constructions. It is only when we have transcended thinking in words, on the higher levels of meditation, that we enter into a different dimension, in which space turns into time and time becomes the space of consciousness, becomes the present, in fact timelessness—which is perhaps a synonym for what we call eternity.

But how can we overcome verbal thinking? By putting vision instead of words, and symbols instead of visions, and then realizing the symbols in pictured experience. For whereas the word limits and becomes fixed as a concept, the symbol is something that flows, that changes at each level of experience, although it keeps its character through all changes and is thus not without a relative identity. Just as a human being is different in childhood, maturity, and old age, without losing his identity, the inner continuity and consistency of development, so too a common denominator embraces the various manifestations and meanings of a symbol. And so the symbol is not further from reality than the word, but closer to reality, and the more strongly we experience the symbol or become one with it, the more we experience ourselves as active and "actual."

Religious symbols, especially those of Buddhism and its meditation practice, are different from signs that are unambiguous abbreviations for concepts or collections of concepts. Thus, one can identify with a statue of the Buddha, awakening in oneself his qualities by adopting the same bodily pose and the same gesture, and so bringing about a similar experience in oneself. In this way we can discover just how strongly our gestures react back on ourselves. For instance, a clenched fist produces an increased feeling of hate and of being closed in on oneself, a kind of inner cramp that prevents communication with others—in short, an "ego cramp." Conversely, the open, giving or blessing hand corresponds to an open, approachable, benevolent attitude that links us to others.

It is undoubtedly difficult for Western people to evoke visionary images of meditative experiences. But by continual familiarization with the archetypal figures of the Buddhist pantheon, the experiences of earlier times and long-forgotten human capacities can be awakened, even if only slowly. Thus a new world of unimagined powers opens up for us, as soon as we make even a modest beginning.

We then come to realize that the difficulties supposed to be attached to the development of visions are exaggerated. It is possible for even the least gifted person to imagine the appearance of spouse, parents, brothers and sisters, children, or friends. And if we can vividly picture a familiar person, we must be able to do the same with the "Buddhist pantheon" once we have become familiar with it. I put the word "pantheon" in quotation marks because the designation of a system of various "deities" (*devas*) as powers at work outside of ourselves does not fit into Buddhism. The "deities" of Buddhism are born of meditation, they are experienced partial aspects of our psyche that have been objectified and concretely depicted in works of religious art. Whether they are gods or demons—as part of our depth-consciousness they dwell within ourselves. Only when we have come to realize this can we understand Buddhism, and Vajrayāna in particular.

For when we then begin to familiarize ourselves with the images of the dhyāni buddhas and their emanations or active reflexes such as Avalokiteśvara, Mañjuśrī, Tārā, or Vajrasattva, we will awaken powers within ourselves of whose presence we have been scarcely if at all conscious. But we will experience the transforming character of visionary development far more intensively if we succeed in moving on to the Anuttarayoga Tantra, where through an inner process we become psychically whole through the union of the male and female principles in ourselves.

This process finds its symbolic representation in the embrace of divine couples (i.e., those above the human level). Here the physical becomes an expression of the psychic-spiritual at the divine level, and is not the expression of a natural physical occurrence such as applies to human beings on the level of the animal-instinctual, and which in itself is beyond good and evil and so "innocent" and, in its spontaneity, "pure" and hence liberating—if only in the temporally limited sense of the ecstatic moment.

Here the difference between Hindu and Buddhist Tantra becomes clear. The former seeks to integrate itself into the events of cosmic nature, whereas the latter seeks to grow beyond this by penetrating to the level of the higher consciousness, and liberates itself from the compulsion of the attachments of fate and instinct. To "plug in" to the driving forces of the cosmos in order to make use of them for one's own ends may be correct for the Hindu Tantras, but not for the Buddhist ones. The Buddhist has no wish to plug in to any forces: on the contrary, he wants to become disconnected from the power of instincts and drives that have driven him around in *saṃsāra* for so long.

His aim is to *see through* these drives so as to be free of their domination. Not, be it noted, to deny or destroy them, but to purify and transform them in the fire of understanding so that they may become forces of enlightenment that—instead of leading to further differentiation (or fragmentation)—now flow in the opposite direction, toward unification and wholeness. Therefore he seeks not power and domination, but understanding and wisdom. He wants not to rule the world but to understand it, and from this understanding to embrace and care for all beings with love.

And so, meditation leads us inward from without, and again,

from within outward. It is the particular function of meditation continually to reunite the inner and the outer world rather than to deny the one in favor of the other. Meditation is not flight from the world but a means of looking more deeply into it, unhindered by prejudices and familiar habits that make us blind to the wonders and profound mysteries that surround us.

Meditation is a state of perfect openness without presuppositions. It is therefore a strictly individual matter that would be stifled in a collectivism and schematism. Only he who can fully identify with the inner image of his goal without clinging the pictures along the way can break through to enlightenment, which in itself is not a final state—that would be equivalent to a spiritual death in total stagnation, and would contradict the dynamism of Buddhism—but a state of perfect transparency. Accordingly, meditation should never be made into a "task" undertaken with gritted teeth and clenched fists. As long as anyone has to force himself to meditate, he is not ready for it. Instead of meditating he is then doing violence to his nature, and instead of relaxing he clings firmly to his ego. In this fashion, meditation turns into a game of ambition, personal skill, and even megalomania.

We should therefore always keep our goal clearly before our eyes, and remember as we tread the path that the Buddha's way is always the *mādhyamaka mārga*—the middle way—that leads between all the pairs of opposites.